PRAISE

From LONGING *to* BELONGING

Shelly Christensen has created an invaluable how to guide for faith communities with *From Longing to Belonging*. The book speaks to the personal challenges and possibilities of a parent dealing with a child with disabilities—and how that translated into a call to action for faith communities. Shelly outlines the need for advocacy, empathy, and resilience as she speaks to individuals and faith communities about the necessity of making one's house of prayer for all people. The book stands on a powerful faith-based foundation that says what's key to all people is the basic need to belong and feel valued, just because they exist. *From Longing to Belonging* underscores the power of personal relationships to help transform people and communities, and how that transformation can impact an entire lifecycle. This is an essential tool for clergy and laity who wish to spread wide their tent of meeting.

> — **Rabbi Richard F. Address, D. Min, Director, Jewish Sacred Aging®**

In her compelling book, Shelly Christensen calls us to become communities in which people with disabilities are welcomed, known, needed, and loved. Through stories and strategies, she guides readers on how best to engage, equip, and encourage their congregations in ways that lead toward real inclusion and deep belonging.

> — **Erik Carter, Ph.D., Cornelius Vanderbilt Professor of Special Education, Vanderbilt University**

"But we don't know how!" is the most common reason a faith community gives when asked about including an individual with a disability. Shelly Christensen responds to this with a highly practical resource fueled by her experiences as a parent as well as years of coaching faith communities through this journey. *From Longing to Belonging* wraps up Shelly's deep passion and extensive knowledge and lays out a practical road map for faith communities.

> — **Barbara J. Newman, Church Services Director for CLC Network, and author of *Accessible Gospel-Inclusive Worship***

Shelly Christensen is unquestionably the "go-to" expert on inclusion in faith communities. In her new book, Shelly empowers people with disabilities to live full, rich spiritual lives as beloved and included members of their communities and enlightens all of us to help make that possible.

> — **Shana Erenberg, Ph.D., Executive Director, Libenu**

In *From Longing to Belonging*, Shelly Christensen provides a comprehensive resource for understanding and developing successful inclusive efforts in faith communities. Drawing on her extensive personal and professional experience in the disability field, Shelly breaks down the components of both the "why" and the "how" of successful inclusion efforts, giving faith communities a path to developing congregations that are more than a place to be included.

They are a place to belong.

I have no doubt that From *Longing to Belonging* will quickly become a "go to" resource for communities of faith looking to begin or develop inclusion efforts and will certainly be one of the first that

I recommend to the congregations that seek consultation and support from our organization.

> — Karen Jackson, Executive Director, Faith Inclusion Network of Hampton Roads, and author of *Loving Samantha*

People with mental health issues desire inclusion in faith communities as much as everyone else, yet are all too often excluded. Bravo to "Mrs. Christensen" for attending to this large population and offering critical steps for welcoming and embracing these individuals into faith communities. She has a gift for story-telling, and her stories about inclusion in her life are particularly powerful.

> — Mark Salzer, Ph.D., Professor of Rehabilitation Science, and Director, Temple University Collaborative on Community Inclusion of Individuals with Psychiatric Disabilities

Through a unique combination of personal, professional, and formal study, Shelly Christensen gifts faith-based communities with accessible, easy-to-implement, practical solutions for including people with disabilities and other differences as an integral part of society. This book brings the day so much closer when people of all abilities are meaningfully included—with a full sense of belonging—as the rule rather than the exception.

> — Stephen Mark Shore, EdD. Internationally known educator, consultant, and presenter on issues related to the autism spectrum

Thank you, Shelly Christensen, for writing *From Longing to Belonging*. Federal regulations guiding the funding of long-term supports for people with chronic disabling conditions are now securing the rights of people with disabilities to live in the community as do those without disabilities. Thus, this book is a welcome guide for faith communities looking to put their values and beliefs into action. By combining her family's deeply personal experiences with spiritual and faith-based teachings, Ms. Christensen provides a practical "how-to" approach to congregations and spiritual communities interested in becoming fully inclusive. As a former congregation president as well as disabilities professional, I have experienced the joy of seeing attitudinal changes lead to physical adjustments, ensuring that all who seek to participate in our faith communities will do so as fully engaged members. One of the most valuable outcomes of creating welcoming and accessible communities are the benefits bestowed upon the entire community in ways that may not yet have occurred to us. They will be brought to us by the many people who will now be able to join us. Ms. Christensen is not advocating charity. Rather, she is showing us how to open our hearts and minds in the faith tradition in which we feel most comfortable—to ensure that all who want to be counted at our table of spiritual riches will be there.

— **Deborah M. Fisher, Psy.D., Program Development and Consultant to Human Service Organizations**

Shelly Christensen has literally written the book on inclusion. Using personal and professional stories, Shelly illuminates the need for and the ease to which an organization can open its doors to becoming a more welcoming community. *From Longing to Belonging* is truly the bible that will guide us to create the sacred space where we all belong.

— **Elaine G.F. Hall, Founder of *The Miracle Project* award-winning author of *Now I See the Moon,* and featured in the HBO film, *Autism: The Musical***

From Longing to Belonging is an eminently practical guide for congregations and faith-based agencies to become communities where individuals with disabilities and their families can find belonging. This sense of belonging develops as they are nurtured in their faith and grow through meaningful participation, sharing, and receiving gifts within the community. As a Catholic and daughter of Abraham, I appreciate the examples from Jewish tradition woven throughout, illustrating purpose and process. The reason for full integration of individuals with disabilities within faith communities lies within the foundational tenets of the Abrahamic traditions. *From Longing to Belonging* provides you with a way to get there.

> — **Anne Masters, MA, FAAIDD, Director for Pastoral Ministry with Persons with Disabilities for the Archdiocese of Newark, and author of** *Pastoral Ministry WITH Persons WITH Disabilities Parish Resource Guide* **(Advocate Publishing Corp).**

In her new book *From Longing to Belonging*, Shelly Christensen has clearly voiced the heart of God calling our faith communities to a "Spirit of Belonging."

Shelly goes beyond discussing the structure of programs-though she does that too—to talk about the processes behind moving hearts and cultures toward a belonging mindset. Leaders are encouraged to work in committees and use inclusive work teams to determine needs, rally collaborators, foster understanding, and launch initiatives. She also takes a thoughtful look at each stage of learning and living in community to foster belonging throughout the life cycle. It is in forming that mindset based on the value of our Creator's design, she wisely insists, that a lasting difference is made and programs become fruitful for the entire community.

From Longing to Belonging provides a comprehensive, practical and insightful roadmap including time-tested examples for developing culture and programs. It is jam–packed with ideas, checklists and strategies. One pragmatic suggestion illustrates Shelly's careful consideration for deep and longer-lasting transformation. "Because inclusion involves every program and project in your organization, there should be a line item in each departmental budget. By following this process, you are ensuring that inclusion needs are considered when programming decisions are made." Gems of such practical insight are plentiful in this book!

Shelly Christensen is an esteemed, thoughtful, compassionate, and unrelenting cheerleader for inclusion. For nearly twenty years, she has advocated for people with disabilities and mental health conditions to be fully welcomed, included, and engaged in their faith and with others who share it.

> **— Lisa Jamieson, Executive Director, Walk Right In Ministries**

From Longing to Belonging is insightful, and offers everyday hands-on strategies to make your faith-based community truly inclusive. I learned from Shelly's intertwined stories and was reminded of many of the anecdotes from being a parent of a young adult with disabilities. How much easier my child's youth would have been if our school, synagogue, and community had had this guidebook as a source.

This book should be a "must read" in training programs for all religious and community leaders. And it should be read by all community leaders, religious or not.

> **— Batya Jacob, Director, Educational Support Services, Yachad**

From **LONGING** *to* **BELONGING**

To Lex—

Belonging makes the
heart sing.

Shelly Christe '22

ISBN: 978-1-946195-27-2

Library of Congress Number: 2018956425

Printed in the United States of America
First Printing: October 2018

22 21 20 19 18   5 4 3 2 1

Design and printing by FuzionPrint
www.fuzionprint.com

Shelly Christensen
Shelly@InclusionInnovations.com

From LONGING *to* BELONGING

A Practical Guide to Including People with Disabilities
and Mental Health Conditions
in Your Faith Community

SHELLY CHRISTENSEN, MA, FAAIDD

TABLE OF CONTENTS

DEDICATION

This work is dedicated to:

All people with disabilities and mental health conditions and their
families, who have persisted in the face of obstacles in order to
participate in their sacred communities.
By sharing your experiences and inspiring us with your
perseverance, you have become our guides on this holy journey.

Rabbi Lynne F. Landsberg, who gave me the
gift of her friendship.

Paul and Shirley Thomas, who gave me the gift of
life, love, and laughter.

FOREWORD

From Longing to Belonging—Are We There Yet?

In the past decade, Shelly Christensen and I have been parts of multiple conversations, initiatives, and organizations focusing on tapping the potential of faith communities to be inclusive and supportive of people with disabilities and their families. We have had the privilege of walking alongside many others from a wide variety of faith and ecumenical traditions, as well as leaders in inclusion and community building. We have learned from them. But we've learned even more from the people with disabilities, their families, and caregivers about the unique and powerful role that faith and inclusion can play in their lives.

Sometimes that learning has come with much excitement, hearing stories of inclusion that led to multiple kinds of support from faith communities. Not every congregation does everything, but if you name any kind of community support that individuals and/or families value, somewhere you will find one or more congregations doing just that. Besides inclusive worship opportunities, there are congregational-based initiatives everywhere. They flourish in inclusive preschools and nurseries, religious education, respite care, adult learning, family assistance and support groups, youth groups, camping opportunities—anytime members of a faith community join together in service to others.

While many celebrate the power of these experiences and opportunities, there is also a tough side. As more attention gets paid to the spiritual needs and gifts of individuals with disabilities and their families, one also needs to be prepared for ongoing experiences that have been as hurtful and wounding as the others have been healing and empowering. One inevitably hears from individuals and parents who gave up on their attempts to be part of a faith community because their requests and efforts led nowhere. Even worse, their experiences conveyed, "You are not welcome here."

Thus, a faith community trying to open new doors and opportunities should be aware that many people with disabilities and their families often experience stigma, shunning, unthinking answers to questions, or attempts to help that they did not request. Even with the best intentions, some invitations or discussions might open old wounds and scars. Being sensitive to this dynamic is the first step that can lead to a new willingness to trust, an invitation being accepted, a new belief they will be heard, and the forerunner of steps that may lead to a mutual embrace.

That hope for belonging, or the lack of it, is what Shelly calls the "longing" in many people's lives. People with disabilities and their families are too often on the edge of a community, or outside it, looking in, yearning for the everyday benefits that come with inclusion and participation most of us take for granted. They want what everyone else is getting. If you don't know what that is, ask the members of your congregation why they come, what they receive, and how it plays a role in their lives.

The best way to get a faith community excited about inclusion is to learn about the congregation's sense of identity, and its vision for who they want to be as God's people. This approach can then lead to a discussion about how welcoming and including people with disabilities and their families will help inform who they feel called to be as a congregation and as people of faith.

We have also learned that you do not start right away with new strategies and programs. You reach out, but then stop and take time to listen carefully, before you try to fix or help too much. You listen to people's stories about faith and faith communities, about their lives, and what they hope for and need.

You will soon recognize that this is the author's goal, drawn from her years of experience as a mother, a parent, an advocate, a program developer, a collaborator, a partner, and a leader who is also learner. Shelly asks us to examine our feelings and experiences of belonging to our own faith communities, then, ask ourselves several questions. First, why is belonging so important to us? Second, why might our congregation or organization want to commit to becoming more inclusive? Third, why might the experience of inclusion and belonging be just as important, or even more so, for people with disabilities and mental health conditions, and their families?

It is only after such an examination that we can start working on structure and strategies. What follows in the rest of the book is an organized guide to what Shelly has learned, sometimes the hard way, from her own work and that of others. One of the reasons some of us have been so passionate about sharing resources and experiences across multiple faith traditions is that we realize we don't need to reinvent the wheel. We may need to tinker with it to fit our situation, but we can learn to avoid mistakes from the people who have already made them.

In one of her stories, Shelly remembers a congregational administrator who said to her, after an inquiry about the ways that his synagogue supported people with disabilities, "We don't have any here." Early leaders and advocates for more inclusive congregations heard that phrase so many times that the United Methodists published a small book in 1986 about three creative congregations titled, *We Don't Have Any Here*. Since then, generations of children have grown up with other children with disabilities in their schools. People with disabilities are more visible in workplaces and communities. The plain facts about the prevalence of disability are evidence that people with disabilities and their families are among us. If they are not in our synagogue, church, or masjid, then that says more about us than it does about them.

A couple of years ago, I heard a story which transformed the congregational admission, "We don't have any here," into a vision for what is possible. A friend, colleague, and parent in Canada noted that someone had asked their congregation that question, and the response was the same. But then the questioner followed up: "Wait, I have been to your church. What about that young man with Down syndrome? Or the woman who uses the cane? Or the older person who sits in his wheelchair in a pew cut-out? Or the young child who seemed to have a real hard time staying still during the children's time."

To which she replied, in order, "You mean John. He sometimes serves as an usher or altar server. That's Alice, who has taught Sunday school for years, and is one of the children's favorite teachers. The older man is David. He has probably made half the repairs in this building but it is harder for him to do now. And Jimmy, he is a handful, but he's not the only kid who is. He has memorized an amazing number of Bible verses. But they are just John, Alice, David, and Jimmy. We don't really see them as people with disabilities. They are each just one of us."

The stories Shelly tells, and the empowering paths she proposes to reach inclusivity, are what belonging is about. In a world determined to highlight differences and division, to prove that some are in, and others are out, people of faith have the opportunity and capacity to say and show, "That's not what God's people are about. Here, everybody's in, if they want to be, because God created each of us." That's one of the many lessons we have the opportunity to learn and teach through inclusive approaches that create places many will call home. The outcome, in this case, the gift, is not only to individuals with disabilities and mental health conditions and their families, but to everyone in our faith communities, and perhaps to our country and world as a whole. It is the work of belonging.

Enjoy the trip!

Bill Gaventa, M.Div.
Director, Summer Institute on Theology and Disability

A LITTLE BACKSTORY

User's Guide for Inclusion—Author's Note

This book is a guide for any faith-based organization interested in learning how to become more inclusive of people with disabilities and mental health conditions. I have interspersed the terms "faith communities," "faith-based organizations," and "congregations" throughout the book to expand its applicability to a spectrum of organizations.

Often I refer to both people with disabilities and mental health conditions, but the term "disability" can also refer to mental health conditions. There was a time when those terms were not uttered in the same breath, but now we must urgently address the need to support people with mental health conditions, as we do people with other disabilities.

In my first book, *Jewish Community Guide to Inclusion of People with Disabilities*, I included Jewish scripture and commentary to inspire and frame each chapter. When I began writing *From Longing to Belonging*, after consulting with colleagues from various faith traditions, I decided to again use texts from my own faith.

I have included quotations from the *Torah*—the Five Books of Moses— Psalms, and the *Mishnah*, which is the code of Jewish law compiled in the early third century of the Common Era (C.E.). One of the Mishnah's sixty-three tractates, *Pirkei Avot*–Ethics of Our Fathers–offers thoughtful insights on why inclusion is such an important value for faith communities.

To enable *From Longing to Belonging* to be used as a resource I have repeated some of the same questions and checklists in more than one chapter to minimize the need for cross-referencing. The forms in this book are also available in the *From Longing to Belonging Companion Workbook.*

Any faith community will benefit from using this book as its guide. The content is practical for all. I invite you to apply the scripture, theology, stories, and tenets of your own faith as you use this book.

Shelly Christensen, MA, FAAIDD

THE SPIRIT OF BELONGING

Chapter 1

THE "MRS. CHRISTENSEN" PHONE CALLS

The "Mrs. Christensen" calls all started like this: "Mrs. Christensen, this is Jacob's teacher, I want to talk to you about…"

"Here we go again," I thought. I'd come to expect the "Mrs. Christensen" calls from teachers at certain intervals—at the beginning of the school year when Jacob was adjusting to a new routine, about six or seven weeks into the quarter when he was on a streak of not turning in homework, and at the end of the quarter when the teachers wanted us to know they did their best but… At first I was apologetic to the teacher, embarrassed for not doing a better job of keeping track of Jacob's school performance, and troubled that Jacob might not be successful in school. I felt guilty. However, after I had time to think about it I began to stew. I became frustrated, defensive and angry. It's not easy to hear about all your child's alleged infractions and failures, especially when his teachers never had anything positive to report.

My first foray into parenting a child with a disability, which was undiagnosed at the time, was when Jake was in kindergarten. At Jacob's first school conference, my husband Rick and I walked into a gloomy classroom, lacking any of the colorful posters and children's artwork so typical of a kindergarten classroom. I couldn't imagine a teacher not dressing up the classroom for her students.

The teacher, a no-nonsense, stern-looking woman wearing a drab brown dress said, "Mr. and Mrs. Christensen, Jacob is very difficult, the hardest child to control in my classroom. He is a problem."

This wasn't what we were expecting. "What do you mean?" I asked, feeling completely intimidated by this woman.

"He doesn't sit still. He can't hold a pencil properly. He won't listen. And his behavior is so disruptive that one day last week I had to keep all the kids in from recess. I made sure they knew it was all Jacob's fault," she said with a glint of triumph in her pale blue eyes.

I was horrified! All I could think was how shamed Jacob must have felt. I know parents think their children are always on their best behavior at school, but I couldn't believe Jacob had been so disruptive that he was responsible for the entire class missing recess. How could any decent person discipline a five-year-old child by punishing the whole class?

While I was struggling to think of a way to dig deeper into the situation, the teacher said something that shocked and disturbed my husband and me even more.

"The next day Jacob was no better. I didn't think it was fair for his behavior to keep the other students in from recess, so I punished him. I kept him inside while the other kids went out!"

I could feel Rick bristling next to me. He held his anger in check as he asked her who stayed in the classroom with Jacob.

"No one. He was in here by himself," she answered defiantly.

That did it! This woman, who was supposed to be responsible for all her students, put our son at risk. Because Jacob had difficulty conforming to her rigid rules, she compromised his safety by leaving him alone in the classroom while she went outside with her other students.

I couldn't listen to her any longer. We left her sitting in her teacher chair, wearing a self-satisfied smile.

I cried when we got in the car. All of Jacob's teachers in

preschool had loved him. They encouraged him to be himself, and always gave us glowing reports, telling us sweet stories about our son that we loved to hear. They described a unique and sometimes quirky, always lovable, little boy. This felt more like a nightmare.

After a sleepless night, we hugged Jacob and his brother Aaron, and sent them off to school. I felt sick to think Jacob had to spend even one more day with this horrible person. All I could think of was getting Jacob out of her class.

I also called the principal at Jacob's school and explained what happened. He did not seem surprised. He invited us to come in that day to talk about moving Jacob to another classroom. He was very supportive, and acknowledged my feelings about how Jacob was treated by his teacher. By the end of our meeting, Jacob was reassigned to a new classroom—and by the end of the day, his new teacher called me to learn more about him. She cared—what a relief!

Fortunately, Jacob's public elementary school teachers worked with Jacob, Rick, and me as a team, helping him thrive and flourish. These talented and caring teachers saw Jacob's strengths, and incorporated them into his education.

When Jacob was seven, he was diagnosed with Attention Deficit Hyperactivity Disorder (ADHD). It wasn't until he was fifteen that we learned about Asperger's syndrome. This recent addition to the American Psychiatric Association Diagnostic and Statistical Manual of Mental Disorders closely described how Jacob lives in the world. This correct diagnosis was a turning point. But one we didn't reach until after the nightmare of Jacob's kindergarten experience resurfaced in middle school.

It was then the "Mrs. Christensen" calls started again. Some teachers called to tell me Jacob didn't seem to be paying attention in class, or that he wasn't turning in his homework. We tried working at home with Jacob, but the calls continued. We went to parenting classes on ADHD offered by Jacob's clinic. We learned more about the challenges children with the same diagnosis face in school. We learned strategies to help him, and for a while things got better. He also had several teachers who appreciated Jacob's wit and intelligence, and who encouraged his learning. We loved those teachers, and Jacob did too, experiencing success in those classes.

One morning, when Jacob was in eighth grade, his last year in the middle school, I was sitting at my desk at work when the phone rang. It was the "Mrs. Christensen" call that changed my life.

The assistant principal called to tell me they were going to give Jacob in-school suspension for *poking a hole in a concrete wall with a pencil*. The impossibility of this still astounds me!

I had recently completed parent advocacy training at PACER Center, the Minnesota special education parent training and information center. The three-day training taught parents the laws and rules governing special education in public schools. I was an astute student. Suddenly the law was a new tool in my dealings with the school.

I was legally prepared to stand up for my child in a way I had never done before.

This "Mrs. Christensen" call flipped a switch—I became empowered, emboldened, and I gave my years of frustration and anger a voice.

I coolly asked if Jacob was in the office with the assistant principal. He was. I told, not asked, this man to have Jacob wait outside his office, and to let him know he wasn't in trouble with me.

That done, I delivered the question that every parent of a child with disabilities should know how to ask.

"If you put my son into in-school suspension today, explain this to me. How you will provide him with a free appropriate public education (FAPE) in the least restrictive environment (LRE)?"

A free appropriate public education in the least restrictive environment is an entitlement under the Individuals with Disabilities Education Act (IDEA), (PL 94-142), the federally mandated special education law of the land.

The stunned assistant principal didn't answer right away. I guessed he probably didn't get much pushback on these parent calls. When he finally responded, he was less assured than when he called. "I guess in-school suspension is off the table."

"Well," I said, with just a hint of sarcasm, "I'm not opposed to consequences for actually breaking rules, such as poking pencil holes in concrete walls. But since you called, I have another issue which pertains directly to this matter."

When Jacob was in his last quarter of seventh grade, I wrote a letter to the school principal explaining Jacob's diagnosis of ADHD. In the letter I requested that the school conduct an assessment to determine how ADHD impacted his education. An appropriate assessment is covered under the IDEA. In my state, once a parent makes this request of the school, the school must contact the parents to schedule a meeting to discuss the assessment and how to proceed.

At the time of this "Mrs. Christensen" call, it was now November of the next school year. I never heard back from the school to arrange a meeting to discuss the assessment.

I explained this to the assistant principal and ended my

remarks by saying, "If you don't attend to this promptly, I'm going to lawyer up. We have rights and I'm sick and tired of you people doing whatever you want to do! My son deserves a good education." I paused, one more question on my mind. "And let me ask you this. Who is watching Jacob so closely they even notice this alleged poking a hole in a concrete wall with a pencil? They should be educating him, not looking for ways *to punish him because of his disability*!"

When I hung up the phone, I was shaking. I was also feeling, for the first time, that I did something that I should have done a long time ago. I stood up and I fought back.

My office colleagues, who heard this outburst from their normally subdued office mate, rose to their feet, clapping. A standing ovation for my performance as "Warrior Mother of the Year!"

Once my adrenaline slowed down, I panicked, thinking, "What did I just do? Jacob is at the mercy of the man I just ripped apart, and I may have done something really harmful."

Getting angry was probably not going to help Jacob get the support he needed to succeed in school. But as years of experience taught me, neither was being passive.

But I was glad I challenged the school. Had they complied with the law in the spring, Jacob would probably be covered by the IDEA and getting the support he needed to be a successful student. The big difference came when I learned about his legal rights.

Ten minutes after the "Mrs. Christensen" call ended, the special education teacher from Jacob's school called me. He asked to schedule a meeting to discuss an academic assessment, and we were on our way. Jacob qualified for services under the IDEA, and eventually had an Individual Education Program (IEP).

In the middle of eighth grade we made the decision to enroll Jacob in a different school district for ninth grade. Although it meant driving him ten miles each way to school every day, we had researched other districts and found this one was more supportive and willing to collaborate with parents of children with disabilities, better for our Jacob.

We knew we had made the right decision for our son when we went to Jacob's eighth grade conference that spring. Ironically, it was every bit as disturbing as his first one, when his Kindergarten teacher blamed him for keeping the class from going to recess. Rick and I approached three of Jacob's teachers at the appointed time. The special education teacher began the conference. "Mr. and Mrs. Christensen, we know you don't like in-school suspension as a consequence for Jacob, so we've come up with something else. When Jacob misbehaves, we're going to give him a toothbrush, put him in a taxi cab, and send him over to the school bus depot to clean buses." Sigh. Yes, we'd made the right decision to drive ten miles to the new school.

Once Jacob was settled in his new school, I turned my attention to learning why I felt such intense anger and frustration from those "Mrs. Christensen" calls. I wondered if I was the only parent who ever lost her temper, or who was intimidated by school professionals. I was not proud of my behavior, and I wanted to be able to name what I felt, examine how those feelings came out, and where I directed them. So I did what any parent would do in these circumstances. I went to graduate school.

My master's program at St. Mary's University of Minnesota allowed me the freedom to explore the parent perspective of raising children with disabilities. I spent two years researching and writing about the needs and reactions of parents of children with disabilities. In seeking to understand my own behavior, I discovered that parents have their own needs on this journey and often react in similar ways.

Once parents can look past their pain, and into the eyes of their child, they begin the journey of hope.

As parents we may acknowledge that having a disability isn't fair. We grieve the child we hoped we'd raise, and our behavior sometimes reflects the loss of control we feel over our child's life. Some parents lash out at professionals while others are passive, and some seek answers wherever they can find them. I've experienced each of these recurring phases. Each transition in our child's life shakes us up yet again.

The one place I never had to advocate for Jacob was in our synagogue religious school. At our synagogue, Jake was just Jake, not a child with a diagnosis or differences. He attended religious school, diligently prepared for his *Bar Mitzvah* and chanted beautifully from the Torah scroll. During Jacob's confirmation class trip to Washington, DC he was chosen the class spokesperson when they lobbied on Capitol Hill. The dream we had for all our sons to get a good Jewish education was fulfilled.

But I was shocked to learn that there were children who were not allowed to attend a faith-based preschool or religious school because of their disability. It never even occurred to me that parents might be told "no" when they inquired about enrolling a child with developmental delays or a disability diagnosis.

When a child is diagnosed with a disability, parents are thrust into an uncertain and unexpected reality. We ask ourselves, "What does the disability mean to my child? What does the future hold?" In our attempts to understand something we never imagined happening in our lives, the first question is the one we can rarely answer. "Why did this happen?"

I blamed myself in the beginning because I didn't know what else to do. I felt as if I had failed my son. After a while, I turned my anger toward God. I needed to blame someone, something, for taking away my son's fair chance at life. Disabilities just didn't happen in our family.

These common threads are woven into every parent's story. I learned this repeatedly through my research in graduate school as I attempted to understand my own behavior, thoughts, feelings, and beliefs. I also learned this from friendships I have made over the years, finding bonds with mothers of children with a range of disabilities.

We are resilient problem solvers. We don't appreciate being patronized by professionals who seek to have power over us and our children. We do, however, look for reliable allies in those professionals. During Jacob's high school years, we worked with school professionals who seemed to *just get us*. They listened to Jacob first, and then, just as carefully, to my husband and me. They acknowledged our plans, hopes, and dreams for him. The best professionals brought their knowledge and experiences, and honored ours, as we built a powerful team supporting Jacob's success in school. *I never received another "Mrs. Christensen" call.*

Jacob never did clean buses with a toothbrush. He celebrated becoming a *Bar Mitzvah* when he was thirteen, and continued in his religious school classes. He is still best friends with his high school friend, Patrick. Jacob capably makes decisions about his life. He graduated from the University of Minnesota, traveled to Israel with a peer group, and is a trained computer technician. He has a job he likes. He is a blessing to us and to his community. Jacob is living life on his own terms with the support of his family, friends, and the people who care about him.

And me? I'm no longer angry. I'm proud of how I have evolved, becoming aware my own needs, and accepting myself. I worked hard to be able to ask for what I need. I will always feel gratitude for the many caring professionals on our journey. And oddly enough, I wouldn't be doing the work that I love without the "Mrs. Christensen" calls. Perhaps they served a greater purpose after all.

Food for Thought:
- Think about a time you advocated for yourself or someone else. Why did you decide to use your voice?
- How did your advocacy impact the situation?

Chapter 2

MORE THAN A HOUSE OF PRAYER FOR ALL PEOPLES

"I will bring them to My holy mount, and I will cause them to rejoice in My
house of prayer, their burnt offerings and their sacrifices
shall be acceptable upon My altar, for
My house shall be called a house of prayer for all peoples."
— Isaiah 56:7

After I outlined *From Longing to Belonging—A Practical Guide to Including People with Disabilities in Your Faith Community*, I searched for biblical texts to illustrate why inclusion and belonging are so important in the faith community context. As I was preparing for a keynote presentation in Chicago, I kept coming back to Isaiah 56:7, "For my house shall be called a house of prayer for all peoples."

Many congregations and faith-based organizations adopted this part of Isaiah 56:7 to frame including people with disabilities and mental health conditions. I wondered if there was more to this particular verse that would provide context for my presentation on the Spirit of Belonging and the Structure of Inclusion.

I turned to Google and searched the phrase "House of prayer for all people." I read the first part of Isaiah 56:7 with joy!

"I will bring them to My holy mount, and
I will cause them to rejoice in My house of prayer,
their burnt offerings and their sacrifices shall be acceptable upon My altar."

This became the inspiration for my presentation, and eventually, this book. I thought, here is the way to understand what it means to be human. In God's eyes, each soul contributes to this world. God doesn't just bring us to God's holy mount. God accepts the gifts we contribute, and we all rejoice in the holy connections we make with each other. In God's eyes, everyone belongs. That is how our communities become houses of prayer for all people. This is God's concept of inclusion. I knew it could become ours.

When we emphasize *for all people*, faith-based organizations often jump to how to include the broadest number of people, without regard for individual preferences about how they want to be included. Sometimes we think this means renovating physical spaces at great financial cost, making broad changes to essential programming or worship, or starting a special program. We believe that doing these things makes our organizations "inclusive."

We can become so focused on the phrase *for all people* that we lose sight of God's intent for a house of prayer.

Isaiah tells us that God will bring the people to God's holy mount, and cause them to rejoice in God's house of prayer; their burnt offerings and their sacrifices shall be acceptable upon God's altar. God's house of prayer is a place where each person can rejoice, contribute, and participate. The emphasis is on individuals—not the organization. We are called to think differently about community membership, participation, and belonging to actualize God's definition of inclusion.

Many faith communities are aware that people with disabilities are not part of the community, or have limited access to participation. Many are not sure where to begin to change that.

The definition of inclusion is difficult to wrap our heads around. In the past, being inclusive meant creating special services, classes, or inviting groups of individuals with disabilities to occasionally visit a congregation. Even now, some congregations consider themselves inclusive because people with disabilities get to attend a special disability inclusion service. Faith communities still offer segregated classes for children with disabilities. When held during regular religious school hours, segregated classes are considered inclusive because students can go to music and worship with non-disabled peers.

When faith organizations limit participation, how do people with disabilities and mental health conditions feel about having restricted access to participate?
What does it mean to belong?

Becoming a more inclusive congregation starts with your own understanding of what it means to belong. From that vantage point, you gain a clear perspective of what many people with disabilities and mental health conditions seek to have in their lives. You learn that having a disability is *never* a reason to exclude someone from faith community life.

Many faith communities provide programming *they* think is appropriate for people who live with disabilities. Support for people to belong means building inclusion into programs and activities already in place for the entire congregation.

Belonging is based on relationships within the community that encourage and empower people with disabilities and mental health conditions to participate like anyone else. Belonging occurs when community members build relationships *with* people with disabilities, listening to what is important to them, and how they want to be involved.

What does belonging to my faith community mean to me?

Take a moment and think: What does belonging to my faith community mean to me? Find paper and pen, or use your electronic device to capture your answer.

What are three things you value by belonging to your faith community? These things should be so essential and important to you that you cannot imagine their absence. Be specific. For me, it's being a *Bar* and *Bat Mitzvah* tutor to the pre-teens in my congergation, chanting from the Torah at services, and celebrating holidays with family and friends.

What three things did you write down?

Imagine your life without them. Would you miss them? How would you feel?

Next, imagine if the things that you value were never even part of your life. Now think about someone in your congregation telling you there's one activity you can attend, a special service, or class. How does it feel to have someone else make decisions about how you participate?

Our communities are not whole until *all* of us belong.

Every one of us has something valuable to share within our faith communities and with each other. We have strengths, talents, and skills to share, in addition to needs that can be met by a caring community.

People with disabilities can participate in any, and all, programs you offer. People can thrive and flourish in sacred environments where the community comes together for a common purpose.

Judith Snow, a writer, activist, and actor, lived with quadriplegia. I heard her speak at the Summer Institute on Theology and Disability shortly before she died. Judith spoke about belonging.

She said, "Faith communities need to remember that my *real* relationship with the world is as a created being in a personal relationship with God. I have much more I can contribute and many ways to experience a fulfilling and quality life in the community. Everything we are can be useful to someone else."

I wrote in my notes: Faith communities must learn and believe that *anyone* who wants to belong already has a personal relationship with God, and wants to explore it, share it, give it, and participate, not as a person with a disability, but as a person who has a relationship with God.

Ask yourself:

- What do I have to do to overcome labeling a person as "disabled?"
- Is it imperative to label someone first in order to accept and understand them?
- Or can faith communities simply acknowledge that in God's house we *celebrate* everyone's differences and relationships with God without labeling people?

Finally, my close friend and disability rights advocate, Rabbi Lynne Landsberg, who died in February 2018, said, "We don't welcome people with disabilities because they have disabilities. We welcome them because they are people."

And this, my fellow travelers, is what makes a house of prayer for all people.

Food for Thought:

- In what ways could the full text of Isaiah 56:7 change how your community thinks about belonging and inclusion?
- How does identifying three things that are important to you in your faith community life change how you think about belonging and inclusion?

Chapter 3

EVEN MOSES NEEDED A VOICE— A HERITAGE OF INCLUSION

"Who made man's mouth? Or who makes one mute, or deaf or seeing or blind. Isn't it I, God?"

— Exodus 4:11

Centuries ago, the Israelite people followed a shepherd from Egypt into the wilderness toward a new future. Little did they know that without God's inclusion, Moses might never have been chosen because of his speech disability.

God made it possible for Moses to fulfill his destiny as the leader of the Israelites by providing Aaron to speak for him. This was perhaps the first recorded accommodation for someone in history. Now Moses could do the work that God commanded him to do. He would survive many more tests of faith and strength as he led the Israelites through the wilderness to the land of Canaan and freedom.

God chose Moses because of the leadership qualities and strengths he possessed. His speech disability was insignificant in God's plan.

The Torah provides us with another guiding tenet for inclusion. In Numbers 12:10-15, Miriam was stricken with leprosy after she and Aaron spoke out against Moses' wife Zipporah. Aaron pleaded on Miriam's behalf, telling Moses that speaking out was a sin committed in folly. Moses beseeched God, "O God, pray heal her!" God demanded Miriam's banishment from the camp for seven days. Following her solitary week, she was readmitted. For seven long days, all the people waited for her to return to their midst. When Miriam returned, all the people *moved on together.*

That is inclusion. We move on together as one people. As we learn from our ancestors, our community is not whole unless everyone is present. Inclusion means everyone has the opportunity to share his or her gifts and strengths, like Moses did.

And when one person is left outside of our community, like Miriam, we are not complete.

To Welcome All is a Religious Tradition

The power of this cultural pillar is demonstrated by Abraham and Sarah and recounted in Genesis 18:1-19. Abraham and Sarah, who remained childless into their older years, were encamped with their tribal group by the oaks of *Mamre* in the heat of the day. On this particular day, Abraham was recovering in his tent following his circumcision. The tent flaps were open on all four sides, and Abraham saw three men approach. When they arrived at the tent, he bowed low to the earth before them, saying, "My lord, if now I have found favor in your sight, please do not go away from your servant." Abraham offered them water to wash their feet and encouraged them to rest in the shade. He told them: "I will get a morsel of bread so you can refresh your heart. Afterwards, you may go on your way, now that you have come to your servant." The three strangers accepted Abraham's hospitality, and Abraham hurried to tell Sarah to bake cakes from the finest flour. He ran to the herd, chose a good and tender calf, and gave it to his servant to prepare. Abraham set the fine fare before his guests, honoring them with his hospitality.

This text is often cited as the Biblical foundation for how we, as members of faith communities, must treat everyone who comes to enter our own modern-day tents.

The gift Abraham and Sarah received from these guests might never have been received had they not welcomed them into their midst with warmth and hospitality. These guests brought with them the promise that Abraham and Sarah would have a son of their own.

What gifts might we receive when we welcome people with disabilities and mental health conditions into our own midst?

Disability Defined

The definition of disability set forth in the Americans with Disabilities Act (ADA) does not distinguish between type, severity, or duration of the disability.[1] It states:

Disability means, with respect to an individual:

(i) A physical or mental disability that substantially limits one or more of the major life activities of such individual;

(ii) A record of such an impairment; or

(iii) Being regarded as having such an impairment.

The ADA definition is an inclusive one that tends to capture both the largest and broadest estimate of people with disabilities. It describes a disability as a condition which limits a person's ability to function in major life activities. These include communication, walking, thinking, learning, and self-care, such as feeding and dressing oneself—and which are likely to continue indefinitely, resulting in the need for supportive services.[2]

Who is a Person with a Disability?

Anyone can be a person with a disability. You, your child, spouse, parent, friend, neighbor, co-worker, employer, or someone in the public eye, can have a disability. Some people are born with a disability while others acquire a disability during their lifetime. Some disabilities affect a person's entire life, while some disabilities are temporary.

Sometimes you can see the disability. A person may use an assistive device, such as a wheelchair, a walker or cane, a hearing aid, a white cane, or a service or emotional support animal.

Sometimes you cannot see that a person has a disability. Many not-apparent disabilities[3] affect certain brain functions, such as learning, processing or remembering information, working memory, paying attention, regulating behavior, or interpreting social cues. Other not-apparent disabilities occur because of an accident, illness, or as a result of the aging process. People might sustain a traumatic brain injury through illness or accident. Traumatic brain injuries can affect communication, memory, cognitive functions, organizational skills, and mobility. As people age, they may experience decreased abilities in a number of sensory, memory, mobility, or cognitive functions.

Some people with disabilities require 24-hour care and support. Others may need accommodations, take medication, or receive physical or occupational therapy to manage the tasks of daily living. Some people have one-to-one coaches or aides to support them at work or school.

There are people with disabilities who make great contributions to the world and others who would, if they had the appropriate opportunities and support to do so. Some people with disabilities have friends, while others yearn to have friends and be a friend.

People with disabilities enjoy being with their families, having romantic relationships, raising families, learning throughout their lives, working, volunteering for non-profit organizations and political campaigns, enjoying hobbies, going to ballgames, traveling, worshipping with their congregation, and making a difference in their community.

People with disabilities want the same things that people without disabilities want in their lives.

You can install a ramp to make your building more accessible. And the person who uses a mobility device, or who pushes a child in a stroller, will appreciate that. But the heart and soul of inclusion is more clearly exemplified when the people in the building extend warmth and friendship, encouraging and supporting people with disabilities and mental health conditions to participate fully in all of the wonderful things that happen in the building. We all want to belong.

What is Inclusion?

Inclusion extends beyond an open door, a ramp, or special services and activities for people with disabilities. Inclusion means that obstacles to belonging are eliminated. Inclusion makes it possible for all people to participate, rejoice, worship, learn, find comfort and solace in times of need, and contribute to the community.

An inclusive community values all people, making each one to feel that he or she belongs. It's a place where people of all abilities come together to participate, share their gifts and talents, find comfort and comfort others, and treat each other with respect and dignity. Inclusion is where all people flourish, based on each individual's definition of what that means.

Inclusion is a commitment to wholeness, where each person contributes to the wellbeing of the community, and to each other.

Inclusion is Personal

Sharon was in her early forties when we met. I had just started working at Jewish Family and Children's Service of Minneapolis, directing a new initiative, the Community Inclusion Program for People with Disabilities. I was hired to work with synagogues and other Jewish organizations to advance inclusive practices, and bring the community together in this initiative. I also worked with people with disabilities and families, supporting their participation in the community.

I visited Sharon at her accessible apartment in a suburb of Minneapolis just a few months after I started my job. She had moved to Minneapolis fourteen years earlier from her hometown in North Dakota. Sharon lives with cerebral palsy and uses a wheelchair.

Sharon talked about the obstacles she encountered to participation whenever her parents took her to the hometown synagogue. Like many older houses of worship, the entrance to the building was at the top of a long staircase. For Sharon to get into the building, her parents needed help to carry her up the stairs in her wheelchair. As she grew older, it became more difficult to carry her. Consequently, Sharon spent very little time in the synagogue. She recalled that she loved the times she occasionally joined her peers at religious school, as well as going to services with her family.

Sharon's parents wanted her to be a part of the Jewish community. But because it was difficult to participate at the synagogue and in the community, her parents cultivated her cultural and spiritual identity at home, celebrating Shabbat and all the holidays.

Sharon chose to move to Minneapolis-St. Paul with its larger Jewish community. She felt there would be more opportunities to participate. Sharon began her journey with hope.

Over the next fourteen years—yes, you read that right—Sharon called synagogue after synagogue to inquire about joining. Sharon's speech is affected by cerebral palsy, sometimes making it difficult for people to understand her. When she left messages about her interest in joining a congregation, *no one* returned her calls. When someone answered the phone and Sharon told them why she was calling, they informed her, "We don't have people with disabilities here."

Sharon's tenacity, coupled with her desire to find a welcoming congregation, proved to be a gift. Frustrated, but undaunted by fruitless efforts, she kept on with her search, and finally, after fourteen years, she found a congregation that was constructing an accessible building and welcomed Sharon.

Sharon invited me to go with her to meet with the rabbi of the synagogue she wanted to join. It happened to be the congregation where my husband and I belong. She was so excited to finally have this meeting.

Rabbi Norman Cohen greeted us at the appointed time. This was Sharon's appointment with the rabbi, so I sat quietly while they talked.

I imagine this conversation was typical of a first meeting with any prospective congregant. Sharon shared her story of growing up in North Dakota, her passion for Judaism, her story of moving to Minneapolis, and her desire to find a synagogue where she could belong. When Rabbi Cohen asked her what her interests were, Sharon mentioned she'd like to join several committees, and said without hesitation, "I want to have a *Bat Mitzvah!*"

Rabbi Cohen asked Sharon what was important to her, and how she wanted to participate in the life of the congregation. That was when she knew she had found her rabbi and her synagogue.

Rabbi Cohen asked Sharon if her parents were alive.

She hesitated a moment and through tears said, "My dad died when we lived in North Dakota, and my mom died after I moved to Minneapolis." She added, "I have never been to a synagogue to say *Kaddish* (a mourner's prayer recited on the anniversary of a loved one's death) for my parents."

I thought about how supported I felt when I went to the synagogue to say *Kaddish* for my dad. Having my synagogue community support me in my loss was so important and comforting to me as I mourned. For all these years, Sharon was deprived of the important process of saying *Kaddish* with a community. How could anyone take that away from another person?

All I could think was, "we have so much work to do!"

Sharon's journey has become the symbol of inclusion for people with disabilities and their families. The stairs to her family synagogue in North Dakota symbolize barriers to enjoying a faith community life. They symbolize the people who live with intellectual, developmental, physical, neurobehavioral, and emotional disabilities—who are invisible to their faith communities.

Sharon does not want anyone's pity. The first time we met at her apartment, I asked her what was important to her. She replied, "All I've ever wanted was to belong."

Why Faith Communities Struggle with Inclusion

Perspectives on inclusion vary from institution to institution.

Basically, many faith communities want to do what is right by people with disabilities and mental health conditions. Often faith communities don't know how to welcome people who are perceived to have different needs or how to minister to them. It seems that faith communities want to get it right, but because they approach inclusion from an organizational standpoint, they start by considering the impact on the institution. However, little thought is given to meeting personal needs.

The journey to becoming an inclusive and welcoming faith community begins with understanding underlying beliefs about inclusion.

As you review these underlying beliefs and thoughts, consider how they manifest in your organization's practices toward inclusion:

- We don't have money to be inclusive. Our budget is already stressed, and we're not starting any new projects.
- We don't have accessible facilities and cannot afford to make any building changes. It's just too costly to undertake renovations.
- We don't have any people with disabilities who attend our services or programs.
- We are already inclusive enough. We don't need to do anything more.
- We don't know what to do to be more inclusive. We don't know what inclusion actually means.
- People with disabilities might disrupt worship for the other people. They are often noisy, move around a lot,

and distract people from prayer and listening to the sermon.

- We can't afford to hire someone to run a special ministry.
- We invite people from the nearby group home to visit us once a year.

Institutional thinking can create obstacles to inclusion. Even congregations that have instituted inclusion committees must still consider institutional obstacles, and how they affect individual participation and belonging.

One Congregation's Story

I was invited to a church's annual Sunday of Inclusion service. The entire service was transcribed and live-captioned. Several large screens placed throughout the sanctuary showed the service prayers and other readings.

During the service, the pastor invited the inclusion committee chair to join him at the pulpit to share the committee's accomplishments. When the chair asked inclusion committee members to stand, at least twenty people rose. Next she said the congregation was pleased to welcome "special guests" to the congregation on this special Sunday of Inclusion. The guests were men and women who lived in several different group homes for people with disabilities.

My host and I arrived at the church after the service had started. The sanctuary was packed, and the only open seats were way in the back. We seated ourselves next to the guests from the group homes who were clustered in the back of the sanctuary.

From this vantage point, things didn't look very inclusive.

While the pastor and the inclusion committee chair spoke, the woman sitting nearest to me started to vocalize indistinguishable sounds and wiggle in her seat. Several other men and women from this group started making loud sounds. People several rows in front of us were disturbed by the commotion and turned around and gave their invited guests what I refer to as the "be quiet!" look.

After fifteen minutes, the inclusion committee chair concluded her talk about her welcoming congregation. The congregation's soloist returned to the pulpit and began to sing a beautiful hymn. Suddenly, the guests seated near me grew very quiet. I turned to look at the woman closest to me, and as I did, our eyes met. Eye contact established, I held out my hand, as did she, and for a moment we held hands and connected in this deeply spiritual way. In this moment, I saw the light in her eyes, the reflection of the Divine, and it took my breath away.

Perhaps hearing the sacred music brought back memories of her own family celebrations or attending weekly and holiday services. I saw her yearning to connect to something so important in her life, something that was taken away from her when she moved where she now lived.

This nameless woman was one of those *unintentional teachers* who taught me the danger of taking something important away from another person. I wonder what her life might have been like had her connection to her faith community not been interrupted.

For this woman, and clearly for others who attended the service with her, there was a connection, and that connection is called "belonging."

Living with a disability must never be a reason to exclude or marginalize someone from involvement in their chosen faith community. When someone with a disability is a *valued* member of the community, and not an occasional visitor, they can genuinely participate wherever and whenever they choose. This is the *Spirit of Belonging*.

The concept of belonging is making its way into our conversations at faith and disability conferences. I often use the word "belonging" to replace "inclusion." We have diluted the intention of inclusion by describing any activity for, with, or about people with disabilities that occurs inside a faith community. And, as I learned in such an obvious way, just being in a sanctuary, or in a religious building, *is not necessarily inclusion.*

Belonging and Inclusion

This book is based on two concepts, both equally important-the Structure of Inclusion and the Spirit of Belonging.

First, the Structure of Inclusion creates and implements all the tangible things that move a faith organization forward. These include assessing current practices, creating an inclusion committee, developing a vision and a plan, evaluating policies, advising professional staff and lay leadership, educating the community and raising awareness, and developing language which reinforces inclusion.

When faith communities *only* focus on the Structure of Inclusion, they become distracted from *why* they do this work in the first place—to support people so they feel they belong. By attending to individual hopes, dreams, strengths, talents, and needs, the organization will become more inclusive and welcoming.

Second, the Spirit of Belonging recognizes that belonging is a human need—and there is no greater opportunity to belong than to be a valued member of one's faith community. When we belong, we have relationships and personal connections, we are respected and we respect others, we feel valued and we value others.

"There are no barriers to God's love. There should be no barriers in God's house."[4]

– Ginny Thornburgh

Congregational efforts should diminish barriers and obstacles because we see each person created in God's image. We see equity in our relationships with each other. We treat each other with respect and dignity. Finally, we learn and acknowledge that what is important to a participant in their faith community is unique to every individual. Assuming we know what is important to another person deprives both the individual and the community of the richness that each offers.

Think about the ways *you* are included in your faith community. Are all the things that are important to you, those things that give your life quality and meaning, present in your life in the community?

The Spirit of Belonging

The Spirit of Belonging is about connections and relationships. It recognizes the contributions and needs of all individuals in a community environment that celebrates differences, contributions, personal interests, and needs. Belonging starts with this question: "What is important to you, and how can we work together to make sure that's part of your participation?" The Spirit of Belonging moves faith communities from doing things *for* people with disabilities and mental health conditions to working *with* people.

The Spirit of Belonging demands that we look beyond ramps, inclusion committees, and disability awareness Sabbaths, to becoming a house of prayer for all peoples. The Spirit of Belonging is a balance of collaboration, support, imagination, and even risk to nurture individual choices that can lead to a satisfying life as a member of the community.

Elements of the Spirit of Belonging are:

- Developing and nurturing relationships
- Listening to people share what is important to them
- Participating in services, social events, learning, leadership, committees, and organizational groups
- Accommodating individual needs
- Considering people, not as objects of others' acts of charity, but as contributors of loving kindness
- Removing *individual* obstacles to participation in all community activities
- Seeing the person, not their disability

The Structure of Inclusion

The Structure of Inclusion offers a way for organizations to manage the activities that foster inclusion. It provides a set of tools to assess how your organization currently addresses inclusion, and creates a leadership team to develop a vision and strategies to advance inclusion, raise awareness, and evaluate progress.

The Structure of Inclusion provides practical strategies. Faith communities already have structures and policies in place to address functions that keep them vital and renewed. Having a structure for inclusion is no different.

Elements of the Structure of Inclusion are:

- Establishing an inclusion committee
- Writing a mission statement for inclusion
- Assessing organizational processes, policies, and attitudes

- Identifying goals and priorities
- Developing a strategic plan and measurable goals
- Identifying internal and external partners
- Developing a training plan
- Raising awareness and promoting inclusion
- Reviewing and revising the strategic plan at set intervals

Advice for Faith Communities

I was a speaker at a "That All May Worship" retreat hosted by Faith Inclusion Network of Hampton Roads, Virginia. The executive director, Karen Jackson, asked me to answer the question: What is your best advice for faith communities beginning to embrace inclusion?

This is how I answered the question. Consider my response as you read this book and bring its teachings into practice in your own community.

- Be bold and audacious. You are not creating a new program or a "congregation" for people with disabilities and mental health conditions. You are doing what you do best—welcoming people and fostering their sense of belonging.
- Look at the ways you already do this and ask: What are ways people feel welcome in this congregation?
- Ask yourself: Why do we have stumbling blocks in our ability to welcome people with disabilities? How do those stumbling blocks diminish people's ability and inclination to belong?
- Examine your own biases and attitudes. Ask yourself: What impact do they have on my perspective?

- Treat people with disabilities and mental health conditions the same way you treat anyone else. Ask someone how they wish to be involved in the faith community. Work with each individual to achieve their goals.

A *midrash* (rabbinic interpretation) speaks to each one of us as creations in God's image. "A procession of angels passes before each person, and the heralds go before them, saying 'Make way for the image of God.'" [5]

Like Moses, may we be regarded for our strengths, contributing to our community in our own unique ways. Like Abraham and Sarah, may we find ways to welcome and accommodate those who yearn to be part of our community. And like the community of Miriam, may we recognize the Divine Presence in each person we meet, knowing we are not whole until all of us belong. May we go forth, each of us, to do our part to ensure people with disabilities, mental health conditions, and those who love them, participate in community life like anyone else.

As my rabbi, Norman Cohen, once said, "If you look in a person's eyes and see the spark of the Divine there, you won't have to wonder how to treat them. You'll know."

I will always remember these words.

Food for Thought:
- Has your faith community focused more on the Spirit of Belonging or the Structure of Inclusion?
- How can your community strike a balance between the two?

Chapter 4

OBSTACLES AND OPPORTUNITIES

*You shall not insult the deaf or place a stumbling block before the blind.
I am the Lord.*

— Leviticus 19:14

One of the very first calls I received in my coordinator role for the Jewish Community Inclusion Program for People with Disabilities was from the mother of an adult son who had a disability. She told me when her family lived in another state the Jewish family service agency offered a social program for people with disabilities. This mother told me how wonderful it was for her son to go to a monthly program for young adults with "mild" disabilities.

That wasn't the reason she called. She continued, "When we moved here about five years ago, I called your agency expecting to hear about programs and services for people with disabilities. The person I spoke with said, "Ma'am, *we don't have any people with disabilities here.*"

A few days after the call from this mother, I called the administrator at a local synagogue to introduce myself and tell her how the Inclusion Program could assist the congregation. She said, "This is a lovely thing to do! But, *we don't have any people with disabilities here.* We don't need your services."

It didn't take me long to see a pattern. According to U.S. Census figures, nearly twenty percent of the population has a diagnosed disability.

How could faith-based organizations be oblivious to the fact that one in five people live with a disability?

My work was laid before me. One of the first, and arguably, the most important task was to raise awareness about the very existence of people with disabilities in our community.

In this chapter we'll explore data to understand why inclusion in faith community life is so important to people with disabilities. We'll also discuss the obstacles to inclusion and belonging. Any efforts to change the culture of a community must begin by examining the underlying beliefs that perpetuate exclusion and marginalization of people with disabilities.

What if We Didn't Know What Those Obstacles Were?

We've tried to diminish obstacles by promoting segregated disability-only programs, services, and classes. We have kept people away from what faith communities do best—bringing people together—while thinking we're doing something noble or kind for them.

We've shushed our curious children when they ask, "Mommy, why is that lady in a wheelchair?" as if the child was rudely telling the woman something she didn't know. We've treated people as if they're invisible, ignoring them, because we were afraid of saying or doing something hurtful or wrong. In our houses of worship, we've turned and stared down a person who vocalizes during a sermon or prayer, as if our way of conducting ourselves in the sacred space is the only way.

We can all do better.

For too long, them-and-us thinking has shaded our attitudes, and consequently, our approaches to inclusion. The "us" mirrored years of ableism; identifying people by their physical, cognitive, intellectual, or emotional abilities. By seeing only what a person cannot do, we have failed to see that spark of the divine in "them," their Godliness.

This reference brings me back to purpose in life and to seeing the divine spark in the eyes of each person we meet.

In Exodus 35:4-36, each person was asked to contribute to the building of the Tabernacle in a variety of ways. Moses gathered the Israelites, told them to collect gifts of materials from those whose hearts so moved them—gifts of gold, silver, copper, yarns, fine linen, goat hair, ram skins, acacia wood, olive oil, spices, and precious stones. Moses invited all who were skilled to build the Tabernacle, make its furnishings, and create the priestly vestments. Moses included everyone to contribute and participate. His invitation stands as an example for us to follow.

Context for Inclusion

Spirituality and religion represent an important, yet un-developed area of life for people with disabilities. Over 250 studies have examined the connection of spirituality, congregational participation, and indicators of well-being. [1]

Approximately 56.7 million Americans have a disability. According to the U.S. Census figures: [2]

- Eight percent of children under fifteen have disabilities.
- Twenty-one percent of people fifteen and older have disabilities.
- Seventeen percent of people twenty-one through sixty-four have disabilities.
- Fifty percent of adults sixty-five and older have disabilities.

According to a study by the World Health Organization

(WHO), over one billion people live with disabilities in the world.[3] People with disabilities comprise the largest minority in the U.S, and in the world.

According to a study by Carter et al., people with disabilities were more likely to be accompanied by friends and family when attending religious activities.[4] Further, when people attend religious services, they are more likely to be involved in other activities in the community. Researchers wrote, "The more limited participation of persons with complex communication and mobility challenges suggests a need to reach out more broadly to all adults with Intellectual and Developmental Disabilities (IDD) to ensure that every interested person has opportunities to worship, learn, serve, and have fellowship within a caring community of faith. Faith community attendance may be impacted more by the level or severity of disability than other forms of community participation (e.g. going out to eat, shopping) and makes this discrepancy especially noteworthy."

What blocks participation in a person's faith community of choice? The study by Carter et al., cites involvement in religious activities as lower than other areas of involvement, according to the National Core Indicators. The National Core Indicators are standard measures used across states to assess the outcomes of services provided to individuals with disabilities and families.

This may be a reflection of how agencies that provide services to people with disabilities develop individual plans for those they support. Religion and spirituality may be construed as too personal an issue for service providers to engage with, or an individual's religious affiliation may be different than the caregivers, making it uncomfortable to accompany the person to services. There is a misconception that faith community inclusion is a violation of the church and state laws. This is just not true! Too often the spiritual or religious preferences and interests are not included in an individual's plan. Researchers point out that unlike in educational settings and workplaces, faith community engagement is not covered under legal mandates, and may be seen as less important.

On the faith community side, many clergy have received limited training to support people with disabilities and mental health conditions. Although some seminaries offer classes on inclusion, the topic is more often discussed as part of other coursework, or not at all. Many clergy are concerned about the spiritual wellbeing and participation of people with disabilities, and are leading congregational initiatives. The Institute on Theology and Disability provides a five-day immersive experience, bringing academics, theologians, and others to explore the inclusive intersections of faith and disabilities. The American Association on Intellectual and Developmental Disabilities Religion and Spirituality Network offers an annual forum for its members. Members of the network have led a day-long pastoral care seminar to provide practical approaches on supporting people with disabilities. In recent years, many denominations have offered workshops and seminars at national conventions which address inclusion, religious special education, inclusive camping, chaplaincy support, and accessible worship.

Congregations still have architectural, communication, and attitudinal obstacles. Raising awareness about the nearly twenty percent of people who live with disability through understanding and eliminating obstacles to participation, changing public attitudes, and educating the organization, are all critical to move to an inclusive culture.

Understanding Obstacles

An obstacle is anything that blocks the way or prevents or hinders progress. The World Health Organization (WHO) defines obstacles as follows: Factors in a person's environment, that through their absence or presence, limit functioning and create disability.[5] These include: a physical environment that is not accessible, lack of relevant accommodations, such as sign language interpreters, large print materials, and captioning. Even more damaging are the negative attitudes of people towards disability and mental health conditions; and services, systems, and policies that are either nonexistent or that hinder the involvement of all people with any health condition in every area of life. Certainly, obstacles impose barriers, or as stated in Leviticus 19:14, stumbling blocks.

Obstacles to belonging and participation occur when people who have physical, sensory, communication, social, emotional, developmental, cognitive, or learning disabilities—are unable to participate in activities that people without disabilities can.

Three basic categories of obstacles to belonging can profoundly impact participation:

1. *Physical obstacles* block accessibility inside and outside of buildings to all activities offered.
2. *Communication obstacles* block giving and receiving information, as well as participation.
3. *Attitudinal obstacles* are fostered by individual and cultural biases, misinformation about disabilities and mental health conditions, and create resistance to change.

All three categories can profoundly impact participation by people with disabilities, but as you will soon see, *attitudinal biases* are the most detrimental.

When you read the rest of this chapter, *pinpoint and write down the obstacles in your own organization.* Identifying stumbling blocks to inclusion is one of the first steps toward change. Knowing the current landscape gives you a starting point. As in any journey, you have to know where that is in order to map out where you're going.

Obstacles to Physical Accessibility

Most of us are familiar with obstacles to physical accessibility. Lack of access to the building, pulpit, sanctuary, social hall, classrooms, restrooms, and parking are barriers to participation for people with some physical disabilities and those who use mobility devices. If someone cannot get into the building and all activities within, this presents obstacles.

Transportation is an Obvious Obstacle to Participation

In the 2010 Harris/ National Organization on Disability survey, people with disabilities are much more likely than people without disabilities to consider transportation to be a problem (thirty-four percent versus sixteen percent, respectively).[6] Lack of accessible transportation poses significant challenges to participation for those with disabilities. Factors include the availability of accessible public transportation, cost for taxis and paratransit, and limited access to paratransit.

More Than a Ramp—A Congregation's Story

The congregation's demographics were changing. Many members were aging, and the congregation was concerned that the inaccessible building would hinder their participation. The lay-led inclusion committee spoke at a board meeting to ask that an architect evaluate the physical plant and submit a proposal to make it accessible. The board agreed. With the proposal in hand, the clergy asked several people to fund a ramp to the pulpit. A congregant whose wife used a wheelchair gladly agreed to fund the ramp project. The date was set for construction to begin, and the board and congregation were informed.

Another congregant expressed her concern that none of the building entrances were accessible. The congregant funding the ramp agreed with her. He put a hold on funding the ramp until the congregation resolved accessible entrances and parking.

What Did This Congregation Do?

The inclusion committee was charged with developing a plan. The ideal solution was to install automatic door openers at the entrance adjacent to the parking lot. They could add more accessible parking spaces. They considered a low-cost solution too. Volunteers could be posted to open doors at the parking lot entrance during services and programs. The inclusion committee agreed that automatic doors would be the best solution, but also decided that a volunteer corps to open the doors and greet people would solve the problem immediately.

The inclusion committee researched the cost of installing automatic doors and reconfiguring parking. The clergy identified potential donors, and with the proposal in hand, shared it with several congregants who generously contributed to pay for the project.

The ramp project took longer than anticipated due to adding the doors and parking. However, the end result was well worth the time it took to fully examine the needs of the congregation.

What Can You Do to Discover and Manage Architectural Obstacles?

The ADA Checklist for Existing Facilities, developed by the New England ADA Center, is a free comprehensive resource you can use to determine barriers to inclusion. [7] The checklist includes instructions on how to survey buildings and grounds using the ADA standards for physical access. Chapter 8 "Assessments— Know Your Starting Point" includes an assessment for physical accessibility.

If you are modifying existing spaces, consult with a professional experienced in building accessibility to identify areas for improvement. Always include people who use mobility devices in your planning. They can provide insights that an architect cannot—and are the ultimate experts.

People tend to think about renovation costs before considering why changes to the physical plant are needed. You can anticipate the objections and prepare explanations and examples of why building accessibility is important. Explain low-cost and no-cost options, and the benefits of building access. See Chapter 11 "Practical Ideas and Effective Strategies for Inclusive Organizations."

Obstacles to Communication

The obstacles to communication fall into two categories: Receptive and expressive communication.

Receptive communication refers to the ability to understand information. It involves understanding the words, sentences, and meaning of what is said or read. Expressive communication refers to putting thoughts into words and sentences, in a way that is understood by the person listening.

Examples of receptive communication accommodations include large print or Braille prayer books and other worship materials, school materials, and audio description of services and programs for people who are blind or have impaired vision. Many congregations use sign language interpreters, assistive listening systems, and Communication Access Real-time Translation (CART) or real-time captioning for people who use English as their first language and are deaf or hard-of-hearing.

Expressive communication refers to a disability that affects communicating or expressing thoughts. Many of us are reluctant to ask people to repeat themselves, even if we don't understand what they said. We don't want them to think we aren't listening.

I was having a conversation, or so I thought, with my friend Sharon, whose disability affects her speech. She began to tell me something, but I didn't understand what she said. I didn't want to be rude by asking her to repeat herself so I just nodded, smiled, and threw in an occasional, "That's great!"

She looked at me in frustration. "You haven't been *paying attention* to me. I just told you I had to give my cat, Goldie, away because I have allergies."

I was mortified! I assumed I would hurt Sharon's feelings by asking her to repeat herself, when actually I hurt her by not listening. I learned an important lesson. Now I ask people to repeat what they say when I don't understand.

Much of our communication consists of non-verbal-gestures, facial expressions, and body movements. For some people, non-verbal communication is an obstacle when they may not understand the subtleties and nuances others take for granted.

Attitudinal Obstacles

Rabbi Lynne Landsberg, the late Senior Disability Rights Director at the Religious Action Center of Reform Judaism said, "Before you can ramp buildings you have to ramp attitudes."[8]

Attitudinal obstacles reflect our own biases toward people with disabilities and mental health conditions. These barriers separate people into the groups of them and us.

Stigma can be the most pervasive obstacle of all. Stigma is

based on stereotypes and assumptions about a person or group of people, and results in prejudice and discrimination. Many people choose not to disclose that they have a disability or mental health condition because of stigma. Fearing they will be judged, some people isolate themselves from the community. Faith communities can dispel negative attitudes and myths by presenting the facts, raising awareness, and supporting people.

Resistance to change is another obstacle that can immediately throw cold water on a new idea or discussion. Some people simply don't have a frame of reference with which to consider inclusion— or they may be concerned about the risks and financial implications of changing the current culture. It is important to discover *why* people are resistant to change. Clearly discussing obstacles and concerns is important to the inclusion process, and this is the only way to engage people in a new way of doing something. See Chapter 6 "Who Leads Your Inclusion Efforts?" for more ideas on engaging people who are resistant to change.

Raising awareness and educating people about their own perceptions, biases, and beliefs is a primary strategy to help people overcome attitudinal obstacles.

Misconceptions and Attitudinal Obstacles

The National Collaborative on Workforce and Disability identifies common attitudinal obstacles.[9] These are often the most difficult to overcome because they challenge our basic beliefs about how we see and treat others. As you meet with leaders of your organization during the assessment process in Chapter 8, "Assessments—Know Your Starting Point," listen for attitudinal obstacles. The assessments provide an opportunity to listen and discuss peoples' concerns.

Other Types of Attitudinal Obstacles

Inferiority is the belief that someone who has an impairment affecting a major life function is a second-class citizen. Having a disability does not diminish a person's value.

Pity/Patronizing is feeling sorry for a person with a disability, or for parents of children with disabilities. People want equal opportunities to have control over their own lives.

Hero worship is offering accolades to people who perform day-to-day tasks, as if they are heroes. People are not brave, special or super-human for living life with a disability.

Ignorance is assuming limitations about what people can and can't do. People with quadriplegia can drive cars. Blind people can tell time on a watch and visit museums. Deaf people can play team sports and enjoy music. People with developmental disabilities can experience spirituality and contribute to the community. People who do not use spoken language can communicate in other ways.

The Spread Effect means that people assume an individual's disability negatively affects other senses, abilities, or personality traits. Speaking loudly to a person who is blind, or to one who uses a wheelchair are examples. Focusing on the person's humanity rather than the disability counters this type of prejudice.

Stereotypes and Assumptions occur when people form positive and negative generalizations about disabilities and mental health conditions. Examples are: Blind people are great musicians or have a keener sense of smell and hearing; people who use wheelchairs are docile, or compete in Special Olympics; people with developmental disabilities are innocent and sweet-natured; or people with mental health conditions are volatile and dangerous. Besides diminishing personal abilities, interests, and strengths, stereotypes can inflate the perception of a person's needs.

Backlash means assuming that individuals with disabilities are given unfair advantages, such as easier work requirements or extended time to complete tasks. People of all abilities should be held to the same standards as peers and co-workers, though the means of accomplishing the tasks may differ from person to person. The Americans with Disabilities Act (ADA) does not require special privileges for people with disabilities, just equal opportunities.

Denial involves believing because some disabilities and mental health conditions are not apparent, people do not need accommodations. The ADA defines "disability" as an impairment that "substantially limits one or more of the major life activities."

Fear occurs because many people are afraid they will do or say the wrong thing around someone with a disability. They avert their own discomfort by avoiding them. This leads to isolation, hurt feelings, and a sense of invisibility for that person.

Nancy Lynn Eisland, a professor at the Candler School of Theology at Emory University, and author of *The Disabled God*, lived with a disability. "Living with a disability is difficult. Acknowledging this difficulty is not a defeat, but a hard-won accomplishment in learning to live a life that is not disabled. The difficulty for people with disabilities has two parts—living our ordinary, but difficult lives; and changing structures, beliefs and attitudes that prevent us from living ordinarily." [10]

Food for Thought:
- List several obstacles in your organization from each category: physical, communication, and attitudinal.
- Choose one obstacle from your list, and list several ways to eliminate or mitigate it.

Chapter 5

THE SPIRIT OF BELONGING

A human being mints many coins and each one is identical. But the Holy One, blessed be God, strikes us all from the mold of the first human and each one of us is unique.

-Mishnah Sanhedrin 4:5

The Spirit of Belonging has the power to transform how we include people with disabilities and mental health conditions in our faith communities. You need look no further than your own life experiences and activities to connect with your own feelings of belonging. Where are those places that you belong? Who are the people in your life to whom you are attached? Belonging is a universal concept, and people with disabilities and those who love them want to embrace a feeling of belonging, too.

Think about how important belonging to a faith community can be. Religion and spirituality often are part of a person's life story yet it is the one area where, as a society, we struggle to help people connect in ways that are personally and uniquely meaningful.

Living with a disability or mental health condition does not diminish or negate the desire to belong to one's own community of faith.

Because each person is a unique individual, one-size-fits-all programs and accommodations are not the answer. Faith communities determine when, where, how, and with whom a person participates by having programs *for* people with disabilities and deciding *for* them how they can participate. This approach is how people become "projects," making them the recipients of others good hearts, kindness, or obligation.

The Spirit of Belonging focuses on doing things *with* people, not *for* them.

Think about the programs you offer for people with disabilities. Separate programs and services may have been in vogue at one time, but they do not foster the Spirit of Belonging. These one-size-fits-all solutions are based on one aspect of a person's life—their disability—and deprive them, as well as their peers, and the community from engaging with each other.

On the other hand, there are congregations that started offering separate multi-sensory and creative services for people with disabilities, and discovered that other congregants were attracted to the style of worship, and now attend regularly. These services have evolved to welcome all who wish to worship in diverse ways.

Dr. Stephen Shore, an associate professor of special education at Adelphi University who is autistic, said in a personal communication, "Take something we call a disability, flip it around—and call it a strength." He tells how his pediatrician recommended that he be placed in an institution as a young child, because he was non-speaking. Instead, his parents instituted music, movement, sensory integration, and imitation. "The first step they took was imitation. Instead of trying to get me to imitate them, they imitated me."

Dr. Shore reminds us that although someone does not speak, they have a lot to say. We must work on the premise that there is always a way to communicate.

The Lubavitcher Rebbe, Menachem Mendel Schneerson, died

in 1994, yet his teachings continue to inspire and guide the Chabad community around the world. The Rebbe, in 1989, told the father of an autistic son who lived in an institution, to put a *tzedaka* (charity) box in his son's room so when he had visitors, he would encourage them to make a contribution to help someone else. This guidance from the Rebbe empowered the young man and his family to fulfill an important role—finding purpose in facilitating good deeds and acts of kindness.

Ask, Listen, and Learn

The role of faith-based organizations is to support people to live involved and engaged lives based on their own preferences, interests, and choices. We do this for people without disabilities. It is time for people with disabilities and mental health conditions to give voice to what is important to them. Faith communities must dedicate energy to asking questions and really listening to what a person with a disability or mental health condition defines as important to them.

Limiting participation and not accounting for the unique interests, gifts, and needs of each individual relegates people with disabilities to the status of the "other." We can do so much more, so much better if we focus on turning the Spirit of Belonging into practice. Just ask. Just listen. Just learn.

Learning What Was Important to Celia

Celia came into my life the way many great gifts do. A friend who was familiar with my work with people with disabilities told me she knew someone I had to meet. My friend was right, and my friendship with Celia has had an impact on my work and personal life ever since.

Celia was a social worker, wife, mother, and very involved as a congregational leader. She volunteered to chair the new inclusion committee. Celia had a physical disability, and used a wheelchair. Many times after our meetings, I drove her home. The time we spent together was invaluable.

Celia was a great listener. Whenever we were together we would chat about our kids, our work, and our hopes and dreams. She was excited about my work as a consultant. We would meet for lunch, and she would eagerly ask about my travels to speak at conferences and lead seminars for faith communities. She told me she was proud of me. Celia taught me how to really listen to people with disabilities and mental health conditions.

Celia died in 2015. She was a champion, showing the rest of us what it means to belong. Hers is one of the still clear voices I hear. Celia's disability was a visible part of who she was, but her essence, her gifts, her strengths, and her friendship made her a person who influenced and changed my life.

The real impact of Celia's commitment to belonging and inclusion can never be quantified. It is seen in people with disabilities and mental health conditions who continue to find their place of belonging in their work, their relationships, and in their participation in faith community life.

I thought it particularly appropriate to talk about Celia in this chapter on belonging. Celia, like many people who live with disabilities, found a congregational home where she was valued, respected, and where she determined for herself how to participate.

Once I was preparing to give a webinar about faith-community inclusion and called Celia to ask if she ever felt her congregation saw her as someone with a disability. Dead silence. I wondered if I offended her. It turned out I had when she answered, "What a question! Of course not!"

"Okay," I said sheepishly. "I was just checking."

Celia gave me an insight. I realized that *inclusion was not the goal.*

Being seen as a person like anyone else, with hopes, dreams, needs, contributions, and the spark of the Divine—that was how Celia saw herself, how she wanted to be seen, and how her congregation embraced her. It's how I remember her. *That is belonging.*

Putting the Spirit of Belonging into Practice

The Spirit of Belonging is based on relationships and conversations when participants share what is important to them. The process is engaging, built on listening, not on problem-solving. The goals are to support individuals in their efforts to engage in any and all aspects of community life that they want in their lives.

Conversations about belonging are a way to plan *with* people with disabilities, not *for* them.

Successful inclusion can be achieved when a person shares their particular wishes for involvement to shape the way they participate. To construct a plan for involvement without the individual expressing what is important demonstrates a lack of respect and thrusts the person back into the role of "the other." Some of the people you meet may not be fully aware of their gifts and strengths, or how to contribute them to the community. Discovering these with someone can be filled with moments of grace.

The Spirit of Belonging is an ongoing, never-ending process, not a simple exercise or a single event. It is based on commun-ication, beginning with a conversation and a genuine interest in the other person. Guiding questions are provided in this chapter to get you started. You may generate your own questions as well as share your own interests and beliefs about what belonging means to you. As you go through the process, try not to think of this as a checklist. The questions are to help you begin a dialogue. You are working together to find paths to participation in those areas that are important to another person.

Belonging is a Human Need

There is no greater feeling of belonging than to be a valued member of one's congregation. It is a person-centered culture change that recognizes that each person has unique contributions to make, needs to be met, and is respected and valued. The Spirit of Belonging asks, "What is important to you, and how can we work together to make sure that is part of your involvement?"

The Power of Stories

Dr. Hans Reinders, Professor of Ethics at *Vrije Universiteit* in Amsterdam, The Netherlands, is a faculty member of the Institute on Theology and Disability. In a talk at the Institute, Dr. Reinders observed that "Sharing the story is an act of communion. The discovery of personal identity is achieved in social interaction with others, and in this regard, disability identity and its discovery is no different. The truth about community is that we need others to find out who we are. The way to find out who we are is to recognize the journey, look back from where we came and give account of who we've become. It's only possible when the stories are heard. The most important thing for a faith community is to take on the task of advocating for careful listening." [1]

Individual stories matter most as we open up to share our personal histories. A simple question like, "Tell me about yourself," can reveal so many aspects of a person—their personal and family histories, common interests, their hopes and dreams. And, in the context of faith community, such a simple question can lead to inclusion, new experiences, and participation in a particular congregation or religious tradition.

The Reverend Bill Gaventa is a pioneer and international leader in the field of theology and disability, as well as the founder and director of the Institute on Theology and Disabilities. The Rev. Gaventa offers advice to clergy and others about having a conversation with someone with disabilities. In a personal communication, he told me, "Trust what you would do with anyone else. That would be a gift to individuals and families. Don't let the disability dominate the conversation. There are so many other parts to people, and they will appreciate those being sought after and known."

Chimamanda Ngozi Adichie is a writer who gave a TED Talk, "The Danger of a Single Story." She said, "The consequence of the single story is this: It robs people of dignity. It makes our recognition of our equal humanity difficult. It emphasizes how we are different rather than how we are similar." [2]

Your own story has many facets. The Spirit of Belonging empowers each of us to listen to others' stories.

Neal's Story

Neal Katz is a performer, writer, keynote speaker, and he works as an organic gardener. Adopted from Russia when he was a baby, he was diagnosed with autism when he was three years old. Neal was featured in the award-winning HBO film, "Autism the Musical," about The Miracle Project, an inclusive performing arts organization founded by his mother, Elaine Hall. He wrote about his experiences for The Miracle Project. [3]

"I cannot speak. For whatever reason, God has intended for me to be mute. Many people might believe that I cannot think, but despite their thinking, I can. What's more is that I listen. A lot of people may stare at me, and when they do, I listen to their body movements and eye gaze. I listen to their ignorance. I listen because I have no choice but to take in the world in the way I can.

Listening is different from hearing. When you hear someone, you simply recognize that they are emoting sounds. When you listen to someone, you actually process what they are saying and internalize it.

What do I think of the people who stare? Let's break it down. What they are saying is that they are unsure of me. They can't quite figure me out and don't know how to categorize me. They are saying that I am not the way they are. That something's not right.

I used to have some issues with this. I used to believe the stares and thought there was something wrong with me. I used to get down on myself for not fitting in. Now, I am much more confident in myself and my diagnosis. I am an advocate for autism awareness, an emissary. I welcome the stares, and I wish people would actually ask, 'What's different about you?' I've internalized that some people are uninformed, not knowledgeable about special needs, and need to learn about neurological differences. I don't take it personal anymore."

"I've listened enough. It's time for me to speak, however it may sound. Through an electronic device, my hands, or my mouth. Now it's your time to listen. Are you ready?"

Spirit of Belonging Questions

The following questions engage people with disabilities and mental health conditions to share their personal experiences, interests, hopes, and strengths as members of their faith community.

In the Spirit of Belonging, each person in the conversation shares something about themselves. These questions are not designed to be part of a one-sided interview. You may not even address all the questions.

Many of these questions can be adapted for children, teens, and adults. If parents or caregivers are present, let the person with a disability or mental health condition answer. Some of the questions may lead to other questions or streams of conversation. The best advice is to treat people with disabilities like you would anyone else. If you are representing a faith-based agency, it is easy to substitute "this organization" for "congregation."

"Tell me about yourself" is a good icebreaker. Just listen to get to know each other rather than trying to problem-solve. Make this a dialogue.

- Tell me about yourself.
- Tell me about your family.
- What are you interested in?
- What do you like to do in your free time? What are your hobbies, talents, skills?
- Do you work? What do you do?
- What events, programs, or activities interest you?
- What would make you feel comfortable as you participate?
- Tell me a little about your faith journey.
- Tell me about your favorite holidays (secular and/or religious). How did/do you and your family celebrate your favorite holiday?
- What's most important to you about being part of a congregation/faith community?
- What activities, programs, classes, services, or volunteer work would you like to be involved with?
- What would you like to know about this organization?
- Do you use email? Facebook? Twitter? Instagram? Any other social media?

- What's the best way to communicate with you?
- What would you like people to know about you?
- What would you like people to know about your disability?
- Are there particular accommodations we can make to support your participation?

Conversation Tips

- Speak directly to the individual, not to a companion, caregiver, or interpreter.
- If you don't understand what someone says, ask them to repeat it.
- Show common courtesies to people with disabilities. Shake hands. If the person cannot shake your hand, they will let you know.
- Offer assistance to a person with a disability, but wait until your offer is accepted before you help.
- It is okay to feel nervous or uncomfortable around people with disabilities, and it is okay to admit that. When you are in a situation like this, think "person first" instead of "has a disability."
- Belonging is the key to inclusion. Let this guide you as you develop relationships with people with disabilities and mental health conditions.

Food for Thought:

- How does thinking about inclusion in the context of belonging differ from how you thought before reading this chapter?
- What can you do to infuse the Spirit of Belonging into your community?

Chapter 6

WHO LEADS YOUR INCLUSION EFFORTS?

Without strategy the people falls, but with many counselors there is victory.
-Proverbs 11:14

Faith communities need strong leadership to establish the cultural shift toward belonging and inclusion. While there is not a one-size-fits-all approach to leadership, there are qualities that a leader needs, or can learn, to successfully command attention and motivate others. Effective leadership can shepherd a faith community towards developing a comprehensive approach to inclusion.

Inclusion may be an organizational value, but when it's without leadership, it is a value without substance.

Who is a Leader?

Leaders come from diverse backgrounds and personal histories. They can be people with disabilities, mental health conditions, caregivers, and family members. Or they can be professionals who support people with disabilities, including special educators, medical professionals, and social workers. Some leaders do not have experience living with disability, but are passionate and dedicated to a congregation or organization that includes all people.

Leaders guide people to understand why inclusion is an important value and responsibility for the organization and everyone involved in it. This is why leadership is necessary for inclusion to flourish.

You can do this!

A Tale of Two Leaders

Leader One: Rose volunteered to be the chair of her congregation's newly formed inclusion committee. She is a vocal parent of a preschooler who has an autism spectrum disorder, and seemed an obvious choice. At the first meeting of the committee, Rose excitedly said, "We have the chance to make our educational programs more inclusive and welcoming for children like my daughter. As the chair, I want us to focus on how to do that." She said she had already met with the preschool director to come up with some ideas for how to pay for an aide to work with her child.

The inclusion committee members were surprised, and one said, "I thought we were going to do an assessment of the whole congregation, and then determine our priorities." Others nodded. Rose replied, "Well, I feel we have to take care of this issue first. My daughter needs an aide, and I want to focus on that. Besides, if we don't take care of our youngest first, how will they grow up to be included in the religious school, camp, and youth group?"

Rose's agenda became the inclusion committee's focus. A problem arose because Rose never asked what the members thought the committee should focus on. Her preschool issue superseded the committee work. People stopped coming to meetings. Meanwhile, Rose continued to meet with anyone from the congregation who would listen to her, but soon people were weary of her demands. The inclusion initiative fell apart. Realizing she wasn't getting anywhere with her issue, Rose resigned as chair and quit the inclusion committee.

Leader Two: The president of the congregation asked Becca to revive the inclusion committee. She was an active member of the board and had previously chaired the religious education committee. Becca was on the first inclusion committee and had observed how Rose's single-minded approach had alienated the members and others in the congregation.

Becca, who lives with a disability, believed in building consensus by listening to everyone's thoughts. She called each of the former committee members and invited them to come back. She then asked each person to share their thoughts about what the committee should discuss at the first meeting.

Everyone spoke at the meeting. Becca listened, and learned that, with all of the different ideas and opinions, one thing stood out. As she acknowledged each person's ideas, she began to see a trend. Members all wanted to do an assessment of the congregation to understand the strengths and challenges. She told this to the committee, and the members discussed how to do it. Becca then asked for volunteers to coordinate the assessment process. Three months later the assessments were complete and the committee reviewed them. Together, they decided to prioritize the findings, hold a community conversation, and create an action plan. The committee was back on track.

Establish Why Inclusion is Important to You

Faith communities want to know "How can we be more inclusive?" Consider this question first. "Why is being inclusive important to you?"

Leaders have to know why inclusion is personally important. It is part of the story they share to engage others to join them. Ask yourself:

- Why do I want to be a leader in the inclusion initiative?
- Am I passionate about inclusion?

- Does someone close to me—or do I have a disability?
- Am I inspired by seeing values turned into action?
- Can I inspire others?
- What is my motivation to lead the inclusion initiative?
- How do I feel when I lead others?
- Do I feel inspired by doing something new and challenging?

These questions help you dig a little deeper to articulate why belonging and inclusion are important to you as a leader.

If Nothing Changes…Nothing Changes

You've heard people say, "Change is scary." Resistance is a way people communicate their fear of change. Resistance tells you exactly what someone believes. When someone continues to resist, you haven't *yet* identified the source of resistance and satisfied their concerns or objections.

Why do people resist change? Resistance could be a response to past attempts that resulted in perceived failure, negative beliefs about disability, or not having enough information to enable change. Many of us are resistant to change because we do not know how the alternative will affect us. Change is adapting to a new way of thinking and doing something. People may feel a degree of loss over leaving the old way behind. Acknowledge this, be patient, and you will be able to use resistance to facilitate change.

Think about a time when you were on the brink of change in your personal or professional life, and ask yourself:

- What was the situation?
- What were my fears?
- At any time did my fears hold me back?
- What was I losing?

- What was I leaving behind or letting go?
- How did I overcome my resistance?
- Who helped me understand my resistance?
- Was there a point I let go of my resistance and how did that change things for me?
- Was the change what I initially expected?
- How was it different?

Leaders understand that they are leading a culture change, one that requires listening to others' perspectives, even when they do not agree. Effective leaders listen to resistance and use it as feedback to help people understand why inclusion is important to the organization.

We don't like change because it's hard to envision results and how the change will affect us personally.

- Leaders don't take resistance personally. Resistance provides feedback so leaders can address peoples' concerns, helping them become engaged in the process of change. Leaders paint a picture, or share a vision, of the destination that sparks the imagination of others.
- Leaders must check impatience at the door, knowing that the journey from the old to the new is accomplished in small steps rather than in sweeping global changes.
- Leaders must come to terms with the risks associated with change and innovation. I hear most from leaders about the one or two people in the organization who resist inclusion. "Too expensive," they say or "Things are fine the way they are." Leaders can learn to feel comfortable responding to these beliefs in ways that reflect peoples' concerns, and

still point out why inclusion is good for the organization and those it supports.

- Leaders know their constituents. Governing boards and staff need to explore an issue sufficiently to trust that a new insight, a new idea, a new way of doing something will help the organization grow. Those involved should ask themselves: "Why is inclusion important?"

People want to make up their own minds about change. Just because you say it is necessary, does not mean people will buy in. You can help people understand inclusion as a communal value that enriches the community and all its members.

The Clock is Ticking

I often say that the clock is ticking in peoples' lives. People with disabilities, mental health conditions, and those who love them, don't want to wait. Every day that passes without action is lost. Good leaders understand the human cost of inaction, or waiting for others to make decisions. Once your organization is committed to inclusion, it becomes urgent to all of the people who have been waiting to belong.

Small Steps Over Time

Change requires a series of small steps over time. While it may seem counterintuitive to a sense of urgency, each step toward inclusion is important. Skipping any of the steps will ultimately slow down the process, resulting in further delays. The sense of urgency drives the initiative. Small steps taken over time will work toward achieving your goals.

Buy-in is one of the most important aspects of change.

Collaborate with professional leadership to discuss who you should meet with individually, or in a group, to talk about the inclusion initiative. When meeting with stakeholders discuss why it's important to everyone involved with the organization, and include an overview of the intended process, as you know it at the time. Then ask for their support and assistance. Keep them updated.

Educate and Inspire Other Leaders

Not everyone in your organization has experience including people with disabilities and mental health conditions. Board members, other lay leaders, and staff need to understand why the organization is focusing on inclusion. Building a foundation for the leadership and professional staff is an important opportunity to advance your work.

These questions create a platform for leading a discussion at board, staff, and committee meetings to discuss inclusion and belonging. Take time for discussion so the leadership of the organization can understand the urgency and necessity of inclusion.

Before you start the discussion, provide an overview of the inclusion initiative.

1. Why is inclusion of people with disabilities and mental health conditions an important concern for our organization?
2. People with disabilities, mental health conditions, and those who love them want to belong and flourish here like anyone else. In order to empower and support them, we must consider the attitudes that may act as obstacles. How do you think people with disabilities and mental health

conditions are perceived in our organization?

3. What is your role as an organizational leader in fostering inclusion and belonging? What can you do, what steps can you take, to be a role model?

4. What can we do better?

Remember when Moses questioned his ability to lead and inspire the Israelites. He tried to turn down God's call for his leadership, but God prevailed. God communicated a vision to Moses, who, in turn, did the same to the people. Moses translated the idea of a Promised Land into a vision of a land flowing with milk and honey. He engaged the Israelites in various steps along the way, such as building the Tabernacle, making them contributors to change.

Moses' skill as a leader guided the people out of Egypt, through uncertainty and fear, dangers real and imagined, encouraging people to remember God's vision until it became their own. As Moses stood atop Mount Nebo, he gazed not upon the vision, but on the destination—upon the land flowing with milk and honey.

Food for Thought:
- What leadership models already in place in your organization can you use to start or revive your inclusion initiative?
- How can you personally help overcome resistance to inclusion?

THE STRUCTURE OF INCLUSION

Chapter 7

GETTING STARTED

It is not incumbent upon you to finish the task.
Yet, you are not free to desist from it.
— Ethics of Our Fathers *Pirke Avot* 2:20

The Structure of Inclusion defines *how* a community becomes a house of prayer for all people. As with other congregational initiatives and programs, inclusion requires leadership and action. Without a structure, your intentions remain elusive, and you will accomplish little. This section, the Structure of Inclusion, is a roadmap toward full inclusion.

Successfully becoming an inclusive organization starts with a group of people who come together for the purpose of developing the inclusion initiative. I strongly recommend you create a stand-alone committee responsible for shepherding the process. Without a dedicated committee, getting started and sustaining your inclusion initiative will be very difficult. The inclusion committee provides the foundation by articulating the mission, purpose, and direction. The inclusion committee manages assessments, the community conversation, and the action plan.

Remember this—no one does this alone. Successfully infusing a culture of belonging and inclusion requires participation by all parts of the congregation or organization. This includes the clergy, governing board, educators, professional staff, people with disabilities and mental health conditions as well as family members, professionals, and other interested individuals.

Step-By-Step Overview
If You Have an Inclusion Committee

Whether your committee has been active or is in need of rejuvenation, take the time to review this chapter for more ideas and inspiration. Committees benefit from new ideas and strategies, and you will find many of them in this chapter and those that follow.

If You Do Not Have an Inclusion Committee

How to start an inclusion committee is included in this chapter.

Assess Your Organization

Conducting appropriate assessments is critical to success. Rather than trying to guess what your priorities should be, assessments help determine them. Assessments are necessary so you know what to address in your action plan. Think of this like planning a trip. You first have to know where you are starting from before you can map out the road to your destination. The assessments in Chapter 8, "Assessments—Know Your Starting Point," address many of the functions in faith communities and faith-based organizations.

Community Conversation and Vision

Gather people from across your faith community for a community conversation to create a vision for inclusion. Participants will brainstorm ideas in an engaging two-hour session, and at the end of this, the inclusion committee will have enough information to develop a specific action plan and timeline. Community conversations are a great way to involve many people in your initiative. Chapter 9, "Coming Together for a Community Conversation," provides details on how you can hold a community conversation.

Create the Roadmap

Chapter 10, "Create Your Roadmap," guides the development of your roadmap or action plan. The roadmap includes goals, timelines, and who will lead and participate in each goal.

Start Your Inclusion Committee

The role of the inclusion committee, sanctioned by the governing board of the organization, is to guide the processes in *From Longing to Belonging*. It serves as your organization's "go to" for resources and information about inclusion. The inclusion committee members are the organization's go-to people, so it is important to have a diverse range of interests and knowledge among committee members.

Committee Members

Invite people with a variety of inclusion concerns so the committee does not become focused on a single issue or agenda.

Publicize the formation of your inclusion committee. Start with a core group to write the mission and vision statements, and add more people as you do the assessments. Once you've identified your priorities and created action steps, you will have the opportunity to recruit additional members with expertise or interest in those specific areas.

The following information is your guide to starting your own inclusion committee.

Inclusion Committee Formation Checklist

Completed	Steps
	1. Make an appointment with your clergy and executive director to discuss the need for the inclusion committee.
	2. Speak with your organizational president about the need for the inclusion committee. Request to be on the agenda for an upcoming board meeting to give a brief presentation on why an inclusion committee is needed.
	3. Learn what the organizational bylaws require in order to start a new standing committee and plan accordingly.
	4. Make the presentation to your governing board. Use the information in this book to provide a brief overview of why inclusion is important and how the committee will direct the initiative. Keep it short!
	5. Ask for board approval, if required, by your bylaws.
	6. Publicize the new inclusion committee to recruit members. Announce the date of your first meeting. Share the purpose of the committee. Ask your clergy and executive director to suggest potential members.
	7. Contact members of your organization who might be interested in joining the committee. Include people with disabilities, family members, a member of the clergy, representatives from education and membership committees, board member(s), and people who are professionally involved in supporting people with disabilities and mental health conditions, e.g. education specialists, psychologists, and architects. Seek as broad-based a group of supportive members as possible. Some people may want to be involved without having an obvious connection to disability inclusion.

	8. Ask that an administrative staff member and/or clergy be liaison to the committee and attend committee meetings.
	9. Schedule your first committee meeting with as much publicity as you can. At the meeting, ask people to introduce themselves and share why being part of this committee is important to them. Limit to 1–2 minutes per person. Introduce the first step: writing the mission statement.
	10. Write the inclusion committee mission statement. The mission statement will keep the committee focused on its purpose and goals.
	11. Share the mission statement with the board as follow up to your presentation. Get board approval if necessary. Publicize the mission statement in all your communications.
	12. Decide who to meet with to conduct the assessment discussions. Assign inclusion committee members to each assessment. Plan on taking two to three months to complete the assessments.
	13. Discuss the assessments results with the inclusion committee. Look for common themes, opportunities, and challenges. These will form the basis for your action plan.
	14. Schedule a 2-hour community conversation workshop to begin developing your roadmap. Decide who you want to attend. Invite people from other committees, department heads, clergy, professional staff, and of course, your inclusion committee.
	15. Look for ways to collaborate with other committees and share information about how they can incorporate inclusive practices.
	16. Organize an awareness raising campaign, such as a Sabbath of Inclusion, or education and training events for each area of the organization.

	17. Although you can support people in many ways that do not require money, ask if there are dedicated funds for inclusion, sign language interpretation, transportation, etc., or make a recommendation that the organization look for donors to start such funds.

Inclusion Committee Mission Statement

Creating a mission statement is one of the most important things you will do. Your mission statement cements why you created the inclusion committee. It also tells everyone else what role your committee plays in the organization.

Your mission statement should be short and briefly summarize the intent of your work. However, it does not describe *how* you will achieve your mission. Use the following outline, also in the **Companion Workbook**, to develop your mission statement.

Develop Your Mission Statement

Step 1: Ask the Questions

1) What do we hope to accomplish as a result of our inclusion committee work?
2) How will the organization benefit from these accomplishments?

Step 2: Write the Mission Statement

Write your answer in a cohesive one-sentence statement.

The mission of our organization is:

Step 3: Evaluate the Mission Statement:

	Yes	No
a. Does the statement clearly state the mission of the inclusion committee?		
b. Is the statement concise?		
c. Does the statement reflect our organization's values and beliefs?		
e. Have we avoided use of jargon or terms that may be confusing or not easily understood?		

Step 4: Write down the changes based on your answers.
Rewrite the mission statement.

The mission of our organization is:

Step 5: Review Your Mission Statement
Ask three people outside of your committee to review the mission statement. Make sure at least one person is not familiar with inclusion. Make changes to the mission statement based on feedback.

Examples of Inclusion Committee Mission Statements

- The inclusion committee supports people with disabilities and mental health conditions to participate in all activities in our organization.
- The inclusion committee's mission is to raise awareness and guide our organization to be a place where people with disabilities and mental health conditions feel a sense of belonging like anyone else.
- Our mission is to be a community where dignity, respect,

and friendship empower each person to feel that they belong and are included in all aspects of organizational life.

- We are an inclusive congregation that accommodates, accepts, and appreciates individual differences, and where all members of our community participate together.

Role of the Inclusion Committee

The mission statement defines the purpose of the inclusion committee. The committee can then write a short series of vision statements to define its role.

Vision: Our committee will:

- Assess the current practices and policies toward inclusion.

- Identify priorities, goals and actions, and manage the process of reaching our goals.

- Raise awareness about inclusion and belonging as it applies to people with disabilities and mental health conditions.

- Serve as a resource for professional staff, lay leaders, members, and participants on issues related to inclusion.

- Advocate for inclusion of people with disabilities and mental health conditions and their families.

It's time to start your assessments.

Food for Thought:
- List three things you can do to get started.
- Name people you can ask to join you.

Chapter 8

ASSESSMENTS—KNOW YOUR STARTING POINT

Every valley shall be lifted up, and every mountain and hill shall be made low; and the rugged shall be made level, and the rough places a plain.
— Isaiah 40:4

Every summer, when my brother Ralph and I were kids, our parents would pack up the car and take us on adventures to such exotic places as the Black Hills in South Dakota and Yellowstone National Park in Wyoming. We never left our house without a reliable trip planner from the American Automobile Association (AAA) in Mom's hands. We knew where we were going, and we knew how, and when, we were going to get to our vacation destination.

I used to marvel at the precision with which we arrived at our destination. With limited vacation time, we had to map our journey before we left home. Occasionally, we would encounter a detour or unexpected traffic delays, and having our trip planner kept us on the right track.

As you begin your inclusion journey you need to know where you are starting, decide where you are going, and plan how to reach your destination. You begin with assessments of your organization.

Conduct Assessments

The purpose of doing assessments is to provide a clear picture of the current practices, policies, and attitudes toward inclusion.

There is an assessment for each area of your organization. The chart starting on page 103 identifies the types of assessments you will use based on your kind of organization.

- Choose the appropriate assessments.
- Assign members to conduct each assessment. Set a time frame to complete the assessments.
- Identify the appropriate organizational leaders to interview for each assessment. Go through each applicable assessment and list the names of people who can give you information. You might talk with more than one person. For example, the "Our Organization" assessment covers a variety of topics and you might interview the clergy, executive director, the board chairperson, and others.
- Schedule in-person meetings. I *strongly recommend* that you conduct these assessment conversations in person. The assessments are designed to serve several necessary functions beyond gathering information. They also raise awareness and build important relationships between your committee members and the organizational leadership. The assessments are intended to foster conversation.
- Record answers and share them with the inclusion committee chairperson who will collect all the assessments.
- Schedule a meeting of the inclusion committee to review the assessments.
- Following this meeting, complete the Assessment Summary at the end of this chapter and in the **Companion Workbook.** This document will be shared with participants during the next part of your journey in Chapter 9, "Coming Together for a Community Conversation."

Don't give copies of the questions prior to meeting with the people you have chosen to interview. These conversations should be spontaneous.

Also, don't allow anyone to complete the assessment in writing. You risk losing important insights gained through conversation if they are given the opportunity to write down their responses. The most valuable parts of the assessments are the conversations.

Assessments

If your organization is a	Use These Assessments
Congregation	<ul><li>Our Organization</li><li>Safety Plan</li><li>Events and Programs</li><li>Worship and Services</li><li>Preschool and Early Childhood Education</li><li>Religious Education</li><li>Life-Cycle Event Preparation</li><li>Youth Groups</li><li>Lifelong Learning</li><li>Building and Grounds Accessibility</li></ul>
Preschool	<ul><li>Our Organization</li><li>Safety Plan</li><li>Events and Programs</li><li>Preschool and Early Childhood Education</li><li>Building and Grounds Accessibility</li></ul>

Religious Education—Day or Congregational School	• Our Organization • Safety Plan • Events & Programs • Religious Education • Life-Cycle Event Preparation • Building and Grounds Accessibility
Community Center	• Our Organization • Safety Plan • Events and Programs • Recreation and Leisure • Preschool and Early Childhood Education • Youth Groups • Day and Overnight Camping • Lifelong Learning • Museum, Theatre and Arts Organizations • Building and Grounds Accessibility
Day and Overnight Camp	• Our Organization • Safety Plan • Day and Overnight Camping • Events and Programs • Building and Grounds Accessibility

Social Service Organization	• Our Organization • Safety Plan • Social Service Agency • Events and Programs • Building and Grounds Accessibility
Grant-Making Organization	• Our Organization • Safety Plan • Grant-Making Organizations • Building and Grounds Accessibility
College Campus and Faith-Based Community Organizations	• Our Organization • Safety Plan • Events and Programs • College Campus and Faith-Based Community Organizations • Building and Grounds Accessibility
Museums, Theaters, Arts Organizations	• Our Organization • Safety Plan • Events and Programs • Lifelong Learning • Recreation and Leisure • Museum, Theatre and Arts Organizations • Building and Grounds Accessibility

All of the Assessments are also located in the **Companion Workbook.**

Our Organization

1. How does our organization's mission statement reflect our philosophy of inclusion? Do we need to review and revise it?
2. What is the mission statement of the inclusion committee? Does it align with the organizational mission statement?
3. Does our accessibility statement invite or discourage people to request accommodations in order to participate? Where does this statement appear (e.g. weekly service handouts, e-mails, newsletters, website, programs, and invitations)? Are we missing any opportunities to publish this statement? Do we need to review and revise it?
4. Are people with disabilities and mental health conditions members of the inclusion committee, other committees, and the governing board? Are there barriers to participation? If so, what are they?
5. How frequently do we communicate with our board, professional staff and clergy about inclusion and the activities that support it? How do we communicate this information to them?
6. Do inclusion committee members attend meetings of other committees, or do members of other committees attend the inclusion committee meetings?
7. How is our professional staff involved in inclusion? What else can we do to create a partnership with them?
8. Has training on disability inclusion been made available? Check all that apply:

    ☐ Professional staff

    ☐ All other staff

    ☐ Board and lay leadership

    ☐ Members

    ☐ Volunteers

    ☐ Students/peers

    ☐ Teachers and teaching assistants

    ☐ Youth group leaders and participants

9. Has anyone on staff attended conferences and workshops on inclusion? Who attended? What kind of training did they receive?

10. Are there additional training needs for any of these groups? If so, what are they?

11. Do we have a designated disability awareness month or weekend? If yes, what are some examples of programs we have done? How have we followed up during the rest of the year?

12. Do people with disabilities apply, interview, and work here? If not, why not?

13. What community resources do we utilize? What additional resources might we access?

14. How does our organization fund inclusion?

15. Is there an inclusion line in the budget?

16. What designated funds support inclusion, and what are they chartered to fund?

17. How does our development director/grant writer support inclusion efforts?

18. Do we use our denominational inclusion resources? Are we involved in a local faith-based community inclusion initiative? How do we participate?

19. Identify and list the steps we have taken to become inclusive of people with disabilities.

20. What do we believe we can improve?

Safety Plan

1. Is there an emergency evacuation plan for people with disabilities? What is the plan?
2. Do we conduct regular fire safety and emergency drills? How frequently? Is the safety of people with disabilities actively considered? Do we have exit strategies in place for times when the building is in full use?
3. Do we have a protocol for asking individuals with disabilities, including those with vision, hearing, and mobility needs, about their personal evacuation needs and concerns? This also includes the needs of pregnant women, older adults, and people with injuries or illnesses.
4. People with mobility limitations may *not* be able to exit the building. What is the protocol for moving them to the safest place possible (depending on the type of emergency) and for communicating the location to emergency personnel once they arrive on the scene?
5. Have we established a buddy system among our staff to assist people needing assistance in an emergency, or any time there are activities in our building? Do we have a plan for a buddy to stay with a person with mobility restrictions so they are not alone while waiting for an emergency evacuation?
6. Do we work with our local law enforcement, fire department, or other emergency agencies to develop an evacuation plan that includes how to keep people safe who may have difficulty leaving the building in the event of an emergency?
7. Have we pre-determined and practiced our evacuation route and practiced how to operate any special equipment needed to evacuate someone safely?
8. Do we test smoke detectors, public announcement systems, fire extinguishers, flashlights, etc. to assure proper function

when needed? How often are these safety checks made? Do we have alert systems for people with vision and hearing disabilities?

9. Do we have a method to notify authorities when dialing "911" is not possible?

10. Who is responsible for managing the emergency plan? Are all employees trained? Are written instructions posted at each workstation? Do our staff members know where these instructions are kept?

11. Is there a card or one-page form that gives instructions for what to do in each type of emergency? Does each workstation have working equipment, such as flashlights for use in emergencies?

12. What aspects of our emergency planning need improvement?

Events and Programs

1. When we invite members and the community to organizational social events (e.g. dinners, fundraisers, lectures, annual meetings, celebrations), how do we encourage participation by people with disabilities?
2. Do we advertise that we provide accommodations? What accommodations do we provide?
3. Is an inclusion statement printed on all marketing materials—e.g. holiday information, weekly announcements, service programs, flyers, invitations, website—encouraging participants with disabilities to request an accommodation, as needed, in order to attend and participate? Is it clear and inviting? Do we need to review and revise it?
4. How do we make people with disabilities feel more comfortable when attending events and programs? Include ways we assist with meals, buffets, sign language interpreters, large print programs, etc.
5. Are people with disabilities and mental health conditions on planning committees for events and programs?
6. What kind of financial accommodations have we made if a person with a disability or mental health condition is unable to attend an event, program, or group because of the expense involved?
7. What do we believe we can improve?

Worship and Services

1. Is an inclusion statement printed on all materials (e.g., holiday information, weekly announcements, flyers, posters, website, service programs) to encourage participants with disabilities to request an accommodation in order to attend and participate? Is it welcoming and understandable? Do we need to review and revise it?
2. What barriers have we identified that could prevent a person with a disability from worshipping with us?
3. List the accommodations and modifications we have made to support individuals with disabilities in our worship setting.
4. What makes the worship experience a positive one for someone who has a disability or mental health condition? Have we asked people about their own experiences?
5. What might make the worship experience uncomfortable for someone who has a disability or mental health condition? Have we asked people about their own experiences?
6. Have we considered how to support the worship experiences of caregivers and family members? Have we asked people about their own experiences?
7. Do we provide babysitting for children with disabilities? Do we encourage them to attend worship services with their families?
8. How do our clergy and other congregants respond when an individual makes noises or is unable to sit quietly?
9. Do we create a "judgment-free" environment, and educate congregants that all people are welcome to worship with us?
10. Do our ushers receive disability awareness training? If so, describe it.

11. How do we let congregants, who may not be able to stand during services, know it is acceptable to sit?
12. What efforts are made to make all parts of the service accessible so people with disabilities can participate?
13. What alternative formats for worship services do we provide? This can include reserved seating, large print prayer books, amplification systems, sign language interpreters, visual prayers, page notifications, and music stands to hold prayer books.
14. Do ushers know where these materials are located? Who checks to make sure these items are in working order?
16. Do people who lead services frequently announce the page numbers and identify the book by color as well as by name? Do we have a system to display page numbers from the pulpit?
17. Is there adapted liturgy that uses pictures in addition to, or instead of, words?
18. How do people with disabilities participate in the worship service?
19. How often is inclusion of people with disabilities and mental health conditions on the agenda of our worship committee?
20. Where does our organization fall short? What do we believe we can improve?

Preschool and Early Childhood Education

1. What is our written policy about including children with disabilities in our preschool? Include the policy.
2. Where does this policy appear? Do we need to review and revise it?
3. What is our process to ensure that we have hired qualified staff?
4. Do we conduct outreach to market our preschool to parents whose children have disabilities?
5. Is there a section on the registration form for parents to identify their child's needs? Please attach a copy.
6. Is there a process for observing a child who may present with developmental concerns?
7. Does our staff understand and use the process appropriately and consistently?
8. What is the protocol for communicating developmental concerns to a child's parents?
9. Have we established a working relationship with the Early Childhood Special Education (ECSE) program in school districts where our students live?
10. Do we develop Individual Learning Plans (ILP) to meet the needs of our students' developmental concerns?
11. Who is involved in developing the plans?
12. Who is responsible for implementing and maintaining the plan? How often is the plan evaluated?
13. How are we utilizing the expertise of lay people and professionals in our school, or faith community, who are qualified in early childhood special education?
14. Are we providing appropriate educational and social

opportunities for students with disabilities?

15. Do we regularly offer staff training on inclusion? Describe it.

16. What is the process for ongoing communication with parents of children with identified needs?

17. What feedback have we received from parents about this communication and about their children's experiences?

18. How frequently is special education on the agenda for the Preschool Committee and/or the Board?

19. Is there a line item in our budget for inclusion? What are the funds used for?

20. Do we pass additional costs for accommodations and support on to families?

21. Do we have dedicated funds for this purpose?

22. What are our strengths in providing appropriate and meaningful experiences for students with disabilities?

23. What do we believe we can improve?

Religious Education

1. What is our written policy about including children with disabilities in religious education? Include the policy.
2. Where does this policy appear? Do we need to review and revise it?
3. How do we reach out to parents whose children have disabilities to make sure they are aware of our education programs?
4. Is there a section on the registration form for parents to identify their child's needs?
5. Do we have a staff person dedicated to inclusion and/or special education?
6. What are their job responsibilities?
7. How many hours a week or month does this person work?
8. How is this position funded?
9. How are students with disabilities identified?
10. What is the process used to determine the needs of identified students? Do we ask parents to share the child's school Individualized Education Program (IEP)?
11. What is our process for developing Individual Learning Plans (ILP) to meet the needs of students with disabilities?
12. Who is involved in developing the plan?
13. Who is responsible for implementing and maintaining the plan?
14. How frequently is the plan evaluated?
15. How do we use community special education resources?
16. How do we utilize the expertise of qualified lay people and professionals in our school community?

17. Does the current educational structure provide meaningful educational and social opportunities to meet the needs of the identified students?
18. What is our process to hire qualified staff?
19. In addition to qualified teaching staff, what is the role of the additional support staff (e.g. volunteers, teen teaching assistants)?
20. What staff development opportunities have our teachers and administrators attended? Who has attended?
21. Has our staff received training on specific educational models or programs? If so, what are they?
22. What is the process for ongoing communication with parents of children with disabilities?
23. What feedback have we received from parents about our ongoing communication process and about their children's overall experience?
24. Is there a line item in our budget for special education, training, and accommodations?
25. What factors were considered when we established the special education line item in our budget?
26. How frequently are special education and inclusion on the agenda for the Education Committee and/or the Board?
27. What are our strengths serving students with disabilities?
28. What do we believe we can improve?

Life-Cycle Event Preparation

Author's note: *The questions in this section can be adapted for individualized tutoring or group training for life-cycle events such as confirmation or Bar/Bat Mitzvah.*

1. What is our written policy about including children with disabilities in life-cycle events and education? Include the policy. Where does this policy appear? Do we need to review and revise it?
2. Is a student's information, such as a school Individualized Education Program (IEP), available to the tutor or teachers?
3. Do we believe students with disabilities prepare and participate in the same ways as those without disabilities? Do we adapt learning materials to reveal students' strengths?
4. What is our process for developing an Individual Learning Plan to meet the needs of students with disabilities in life-cycle event planning and preparation?
5. How do we utilize the expertise of qualified lay people and professionals in our school community?
6. Are we willing and able to adapt the individual life-cycle (e.g., *Bar/Bat Mitzvah, faith affirmation*) service to meet a student's needs and capitalize on strengths and interests?
7. What accommodations and/or modifications have been made to modify the training, program participation, and the actual service?
8. What kind of training has been provided to *all* tutors and teaching staff to work with students with disabilities?
9. What is the process for ongoing communication with parents as their child is preparing for the life-cycle event?

10. What feedback have we received from parents and their children during preparation, and following the event?
11. What academic and social supports do we provide for students following the event (e.g. continuing education, youth group participation, camping)?
12. What are our strengths in providing meaningful participation in the experience for students with disabilities?
13. What do we believe we can improve?

Youth Groups

1. Do we have a statement on all marketing materials for youth group events and programs inviting participants with disabilities to request accommodations in order to participate? Is it clear and comprehensive? Do we need to review and revise it?
2. Does our registration form provide a section for parents to indicate that their child has a disability or mental health condition?
3. How do we communicate with parents about the importance of sharing this information with us?
4. What is our process to learn more about an individual's interests, talents, strengths, and need for accommodations to support their engaged participation?
5. Do we meet with participants who have disabilities and their parents to develop a plan for their participation?
6. Do we have a list of community disability resources? Is it easily accessible to staff?
7. Has our youth staff attended disability and mental health awareness training? What kind of training was it?
8. Have youth group leaders and participants been involved in disability and mental health awareness training?
9. Do we discuss disabilities and mental health conditions with our teens?
10. What is our process for parent communication during the child's participation in our programs?
11. How do we measure successful participation?
12. Who is required to give feedback on the experience after the program ends?

13. Do we document the effectiveness of the inclusion process? Do we reflect on what worked, what did not work, and what we can improve next time?

14. What process do we follow to managing challenges or conflicts?

15. How do we evaluate safety needs for each individual?

16. How do we fund inclusion?

17. Have we contacted our national faith organization to determine what resources are available? What resources have we used?

18. Do members with disabilities have access to opportunities to develop as future leaders of the youth group?

19. Are teens with disabilities and mental health conditions involved in leadership?

20. Are individuals with disabilities and mental health conditions offered the opportunity to attend state, regional, and national conferences and conventions?

21. Are individuals with disabilities encouraged to participate in the same missions, study abroad (e.g., high school experiences) or participate in other activities as their peers without disabilities? What obstacles might prevent someone from participating?

22. Is there a line item in our youth budget for inclusion? What factors were considered when we established this? Do we need to review this?

23. What do we believe we can improve?

Day and Overnight Camping

1. What is our written policy about including children with disabilities in our camp community? Include the policy. Where does this policy appear? Do we need to review and revise it?
2. What is our process to hire qualified staff?
3. Do we intentionally market our programs to parents whose children have disabilities or mental health conditions?
4. Is there a section on the registration form for parents to indicate their child has a disability or mental health condition and requires accommodations in order to participate?
5. What is our process to learn more about individual interests, talents, strengths, and needs for accommodations in order to support their engaged participation?
6. Do we meet with campers and their parents to create an individualized plan?
7. Do we have a designated staff person employed year round who is trained in inclusion? Do we have a designated staff person employed seasonally who is trained in inclusion? Include the job description.
8. Have we clearly identified this staff member to both participants and the rest of the staff?
9. Do we conduct intake interviews with all participants who have disabilities and their parents or caregivers to determine the appropriate support needed? Do we have a release form for them to sign so our staff can talk with teachers, therapists, and medical providers?
10. How do we determine appropriate accommodations for each individual?

11. Are all physical spaces including waterfront, bunks, dining hall, classrooms, exercise facilities, theatre, playground, and other programming areas accessible?

12. What is our plan to recruit staff to serve as inclusion facilitators?

13. What is our process for training all staff on disability and mental health awareness, understanding and managing behavior, bullying, conflict management, peer meetings, etc.?

14. What additional training do we provide for staff members who are working as inclusion support staff/facilitators?

15. What process do we follow to address behavior concerns and conflicts between campers?

16. How do we evaluate the safety needs of each individual?

17. Do we have a list of community resources? Is it easily accessible to staff?

18. How do we evaluate individual participation?

19. Who is required to give feedback on the experience after the camp session is over? How do we use this feedback (e.g., parent communication, training and planning for subsequent participation, policy changes)?

20. Do we evaluate and document how inclusion processes work? How do we use this information to improve the program?

21. How do we fund the inclusion staff?

22. What adaptive equipment do we have (e.g. pool lifts, adaptive paddles, saddles, horse mounts)?

23. What do we believe we can improve?

Lifelong Learning

1. Is there a policy regarding inclusion of people with disabilities in our written and online adult education program information? Please include. Do we need to review and revise it?
2. Is there a section to request accommodations on registration forms?
3. What accommodations have we made for adults with disabilities?
4. Do we consider the needs of potential participants with disabilities when planning and implementing programming?
5. How do we utilize the expertise of qualified lay people and professionals in our community?
6. Do people with disabilities participate in religious education classes, *Torah* or Bible study, and other related opportunities? Are there any obstacles to participation?
7. How do the programs provide educational and social opportunities?
8. What supports are in place to meet the educational needs of adults with disabilities?
9. When planning a program, do we schedule it in an accessible classroom or location? What can we do to make sure all programs and classes are accessible?
10. What is the process for participants to evaluate their experiences?
11. Do we have a line item in our budget for accommodations?
12. Do instructors prepare their presentations using a variety of teaching strategies (e.g. visual, auditory, kinesthetic)? Are materials available in alternative formats (e.g. Braille, large

print, screen reader accessible)?

13. Is the study of inclusion part of our adult education curriculum?

14. What do we believe we can improve?

Recreation and Leisure

1. What is our written policy about including children, teens, and adults with disabilities in our recreational and leisure activities? Include the policy. Where does this policy appear? Do we need to review and revise it?
2. Do we promote our programs to people with disabilities, parents or caregivers, and service providers?
3. Are all physical spaces, including dining facilities, classrooms, gym, exercise facility, theatre, playground, multi-purpose rooms, and other programming areas accessible?
4. Do we have a separate fitness programs for people with disabilities?
5. How are people with disabilities included in the general fitness classes and programs? Do we offer discounts to people with disabilities to participate in our programs?
6. Is there a section on the registration form to request accommodations in order to participate?
7. What is our process to learn more about individuals' interests, talents, strengths, and needs for accommodations in order to support their engaged participation?
8. Do we meet with participants who have disabilities and their caregivers, if applicable, to develop an individualized plan for participation?
9. Do we have a release form for individuals or caregivers to sign so our staff can talk with teachers, therapists, and medical providers?
10. How do we determine appropriate accommodations for each individual?

11. Is there a designated staff person who is trained in inclusion? Is this person employed year round or seasonally? How do we fund inclusion positions? Include the job description.
12. Have we clearly identified this staff member to both participants and the rest of the staff?
13. What is our plan to recruit staff to serve as inclusion facilitators?
14. What is our process for training all staff on disability and mental health awareness, managing behavior, bullying, conflict management, or peer meetings, etc.?
15. What additional training do we provide for staff members who are working as inclusion support staff /facilitators?
16. How do we evaluate the safety needs of each individual?
17. Do we have a list of community resources? Is it easily accessible to staff?
18. Do we provide childcare to children with disabilities while their parents attend our programs?
19. How do we evaluate individual participation?
20. Who is required to give feedback on the experience after the program is over? How do we use this feedback (e.g. do we communicate the findings to participants and caregivers, do we use it in training and planning for subsequent participation, policy changes)?
21. Do we evaluate and document how inclusion processes work? How do we use this information to improve the program?
22. Have we purchased, or do we know where to obtain, adaptive equipment such as visual calendars, portable ramps, etc.?
23. What do we believe we can improve?

Social Service Organization

1. Are all our programs and services accessible to people with disabilities?
2. Do we have an established disability and mental health services/inclusion program or department?
3. How does this department serve people with disabilities and mental health conditions? How many people are employed in this department? What is their role? Who else in our organization is involved with this department/program?
4. Do we receive government funding to provide services to people with disabilities and mental health conditions?
5. Do we provide transportation services for people with disabilities? Do we own an accessible bus, utilize volunteers, and/or provide ride vouchers for accessible transportation? How do we fund transportation?
6. Do we collaborate with other organizations in our community to support people with disabilities and mental health conditions? Which organizations are they, and how do we collaborate with them?
7. How do we involve people with disabilities and mental health conditions in the following areas: leadership, programming, volunteering, and employment?
8. Describe specific programs for people with disabilities or mental health conditions, if any exist. Could these programs be offered to our entire membership or community?
9. How can people who participate in separate programs join programs that are open to the entire membership?
10. What kind of partnership or support do we receive from our national organization?
11. What do we believe we can improve?

Grant-Making Organization

1. Do we require all grant applicants to demonstrate inclusive practices in their applications, including employment, service delivery, training, leadership, and volunteering? Include a sample grant application form.
2. Do we follow inclusive practices in our own leadership, employment practices, staff training, and meetings?
3. When hosting an event, do we include an accommodations request statement?
4. Are outside events held in accessible facilities?
5. Do we offer training sessions for grantees on inclusion, accommodations, and promoting inclusion in their program materials?
6. Have we discussed inclusion in grant-making practices with our colleagues from other foundations or philanthropic entities?
7. What do we believe we can improve?

College Campus or Faith-Based Community Organizations

1. How do we encourage people with disabilities to request accommodations in order to participate in our programming?
2. Are people with disabilities and mental health conditions involved as leaders and volunteers?
3. What are the obstacles to participation for people with disabilities?
4. What kind of training or programs have we offered to raise awareness about inclusion, disability, and mental health?
5. What kind of partnership or support do we receive from our national organization such as training modules, national or regional conference sessions, communications about inclusion, consulting, etc.?
6. For College Campus Organizations – How do we partner or receive support from the university disability support services and academic degree programs including special education, social work, etc.?
7. What do we believe we can improve?

Museums, Theaters, and Arts Programs

1. Describe the training we provide to docents, ushers, and staff to welcome and accommodate people with disabilities and mental health conditions.
2. Do we have a designated disability services department? How many people work in this department?
3. Do we provide sign language interpreters/deaf blind interpreters, captioning, specific accommodated performances, audio descriptions, large print materials, assistive listening devices, etc. when requested by participants or audience members?
4. What do we do to provide opportunities for people with disabilities and mental health conditions to volunteer or work for our organization?
5. How do we include people with disabilities in social and fundraising events? Are people with disabilities on planning committees for these events?
6. Do we collaborate with other faith-based and/or secular organizations to serve people with disabilities and mental health conditions?
7. What opportunities do we provide in our education programs for people with disabilities? Have we included people without disabilities in this programming as well?
8. Have we sponsored any events that highlight the lives and/or talents of people with disabilities and mental health conditions in shows, performances, etc.?
9. What do we believe we can improve?

Building and Grounds Accessibility

When we talk about inclusion and accessibility, many of us think about making architectural and physical changes. Many faith communities start by tallying the costs of adding a ramp or elevator and remodeling communal spaces. These renovations often come with hefty price tags, particularly for many older structures.

The previous assessments focused on practices, policies, and attitudes. The following section will help you assess physical accessibility in your building and grounds. You will find ideas to increase accessibility by incorporating low-cost and no-cost accommodations in Chapter 11, "Practical Ideas and Effective Strategies for Inclusive Organizations."

When assessing the physical plant, invite an architect familiar with the Americans with Disabilities Act (ADA)—or the appropriate regulations if you live outside the United States—to incorporate accessibility in your plans. You can also get a building access survey from your state disability accessibility office. Ask if they will provide training on how you can conduct a building access survey, and if so, invite other faith-based organizations to attend.

The Basics of Building Access

These are some of the areas to assess as you determine the accessibility of the physical plant. The ADA Checklist for Existing Facilities provides a comprehensive assessment[1].

Parking and Paths

- Curb cuts to sidewalks and ramps to entrances
- Pathways at least 48" wide, with a slope of no more than 5"
- Level resting space of 5x5 feet around doors

- Marked accessible parking spaces close to accessible entrances

Ramps and Stairs

- Ramps, a minimum of 36" wide, extending one foot for every inch of rise, a 1:12 ratio, e.g. an 8" step requires an 8 foot ramp
- Handrails on at least one side of the ramp must extend 32 inches above the surface
- Protection from rain and snow and non-skid surfaces are required on ramps
- Stairs with handrails on both sides 32" above the step, and extending a foot beyond the top and bottom of the stairs
- Stairs must have rubber treads
- Slightly raised abrasive strips on top steps to warn people with limited sight about stairs

Doors and Doorways

- Door openings 32" wide or more
- Doors which can be opened by exerting no more than five pounds of pressure
- Doors which can be opened electrically by pushing a button
- Lever handles or push bars

Worship Space

- Seating space with extra leg room for people using crutches, walkers, braces, or casts

- Scattered spaces or pew cuts so people who use wheelchairs can sit in the main body of the congregation and not in the aisles—pew cuts can easily be made by shortening several pews by 36"
- Choir area allowing access to people who use wheelchairs
- Adequate reading light directed on the face of the speaker for those who read lips, as well as adequate general lighting in the sanctuary
- Bookstands or lapboards available for those unable to hold prayer books, bibles, commentaries, and hymnals

Restroom Facilities

- At least one accessible bathroom, ideally one on each floor, which may be unisex as in an airplane or home
- One toilet stall 36" wide, with 48" clear depth from door closing to front of commode and a 32" door that swings out
- Ideally, the stall should be 5x5 feet, with a 32" door that swings out and two grab bars, one adjacent to the commode and one behind the commode, to facilitate side transfer from a wheelchair
- A hospital or shower curtain providing privacy for wheelchair users, if metal dividers are removed and other renovations are not possible at the moment
- A sink with 29" of clearance from floor to bottom of the sink
- Towel dispensers no higher than 40" from the floor
- Lever-type faucet controls and hardware on the doors

Water Fountains

- A water fountain basin should be no more than 36" from the floor, easily operated from wheelchairs
- As an interim measure, place a supply of paper cups next to the water fountain or water cooler

Elevators and Lifts

- Elevator or chair lifts should be available to ensure access to all major program areas
- Controls placed at 54" or less from the elevator floor, reachable from a wheelchair
- Braille plaques on elevator control panels
- Handrail on at least one side 32" from the floor

Assessment Summary

Use the Assessment Summary on the following pages to organize the results. Check the assessments you have conducted. Then, use *What We Do Now* to summarize the practices to date in the five categories—Communication, Policies, Resources, Training/Support, and Participation. List these on a separate page. Then, follow the same process using *What Can We Improve?* Be sure to share your results before the community conversation participants at least a week before the actual workshop. With this information in hand, it's time to hold a community conversation.

The Assessment Summary form is also available in the **Companion Workbook.**

Assessment Summary

Assessment Timeframe: Started: Completed:

Date of Summary:

Check completed assessments:

☐ Our Organization	☐ Safety Plan	☐ Events and Programs	☐ Worship and Services
☐ Preschool/ Early Childhood Education	☐ Religious Education	☐ Life-Cycle Event Preparation	☐ Youth Groups
☐ Day and Overnight Camping	☐ Lifelong Learning	☐ Recreation and Leisure	☐ Social Service Organization
☐ Grant- Making Organization	☐ College Campus *or* Faith-Based Fraternal Organizations	☐ Museums, Theatres, and Arts Programs	☐ Building and Grounds Accessibility

What We Do Now

Communication	Policies	Resources	Training/Support	Participation
List how we currently inform the organization about inclusion	List current policies that support participation and inclusion	List all the resources we currently use	List staff training and awareness-raising initiatives	Include ways we encourage and support people to participate as they choose

What Can We Improve?

Communication	Policies	Resources	Training/Support	Participation
List all the potential ways we can inform the organization about inclusion	List potential policies that will further encourage participation and inclusion	List potential resources we can use (e.g. financial, staff, volunteers, community, online)	List possible staff training needs and awareness-raising initiatives	List potential ways we can encourage and support people to participate as they choose

Food for Thought:
- How did the assessment process create a foundation for the work of the inclusion committee?
- How will *you* continue to build on that foundation?

Chapter 9

COMING TOGETHER FOR A COMMUNITY CONVERSATION

Behold how good and how pleasant it is that people dwell together.
— Psalm 133

Now that you have completed the assessments, you are ready to take the next step—holding a community conversation. The purpose of a community conversation is 1) to create your vision for inclusion, and 2) identify priorities for the action plan or roadmap, as discussed in Chapter 10, "Create Your Roadmap."

What is a Community Conversation?

A community conversation is an effective way to bring a diverse group of participants together to discuss a particular issue. Community conversations encourage both dialogue and creative solutions to an issue or concern.

At a conference I attended, Jennifer Bumble, a doctoral student at Vanderbilt University, gave a presentation on the work she has been doing around community conversations in faith communities. I was intrigued by the possibilities of inviting a diverse group of faith community members to engage in a conversation about inclusion.

With Jennifer's guidance, I eagerly read the published guide, "Launching Inclusive Efforts Through Community Conversations: A Practical Guide for Families, Services, Providers, and Community."[1] I was not surprised to see that one of the authors is

Dr. Erik Carter of Vanderbilt University. Dr. Carter's research and work in faith community inclusion of people with disabilities has influenced me and many of my colleagues.

Overview of the Community Conversation
- The community conversation should be no more than two hours long, and is made up of three small group rounds of discussion plus a large group discussion at the end.
- The facilitator provides an overview before the first round, keeps track of time, and leads the large group discussion.
- Table hosts facilitate small group conversations, keeping track of time, and taking notes.
- At tables, small groups of participants discuss a specific question and then brainstorm ideas. At the end of the first round, they move to another table with different people to discuss the same question. Participants change tables again for round three, and a new discussion question is introduced by the table hosts. At the end of the third round, everyone participates in a large group conversation.
- Following the community conversation, organizers follow up with participants, thanking them for participating, sharing the results, and inviting them to continue their involvement in the inclusion initiative.

Focus and Questions
Begin with a vision of what you want to accomplish as your focus. Start with this statement and make it your own:

We are a community that welcomes and includes people with disabilities and mental health conditions to participate in congregational/community life like anyone else.

Once you have written your focus statement, the two questions you pose during the community conversation generate ideas, resources, and strategies that move your organization toward the vision.

Make a list of questions. Avoid "why" questions such as "why is inclusion important to our organization?" This type of question does not guide discussions toward actions that support the vision. Instead, use "what" and "how" questions.

The first question for rounds one and two could be:

What would our congregation/community look like when people with disabilities and mental health conditions are included?

The second question for round three could be:

What can we do in the next six months to ensure that people with disabilities and mental health conditions can participate in the full scope of community life?

Organize a Community Conversation

- Decide who will organize the community conversation, and what their responsibilities will be.

- Choose the date for the community conversation before you begin the assessment meetings in Chapter 8. The date should be far enough in advance to give the inclusion committee time to finish and summarize the assessments. Check the calendar to avoid scheduling conflicts.

- Schedule two hours for the community conversation.

- Choose a location that is accessible, comfortable, and free from distractions. Make sure the space can accommodate four to five people sitting around several small tables. If small tables aren't available, bring in card tables—or arrange chairs in circles of four to five.

- Determine the following.
  - o Who will organize the community conversation and handle the details?
  - o Who will be the facilitator? Is it someone from your organization or an outside facilitator?
  - o Who will handle the RSVPs?
  - o Who will be the contact person for questions and accommodation requests?
  - o Who will be the table hosts?
  - o What food and beverages will you serve—snacks, desserts, pot luck?
- Decide who to invite to participate in the community conversation. Participants should include people with disabilities and mental health conditions, family members, inclusion committee members, clergy, the religious education director, executive director, department heads, lay leaders, as well as everyone who participated in the assessments.
- Follow up with phone calls to the people invited to the community conversation.

Invitations and Marketing

- Set the RSVP date at least a week before the community conversation. Include information how a participant can make an accommodation request.
- Create an invitation to send via email or through a free electronic invitation service to the people on your list.
- Publicize the upcoming community conversation often to draw from people who may not have a close tie to disabilities, mental health conditions, or inclusion, but may be interested in participating.

Materials for the Community Conversation Include

- Colored markers, pens, pencils.
- White placemats at each seat—enough so participants can use a new placemat for each of the three rounds.
- Flipchart paper, tape, and markers to record results during the large group discussion.
- Notepaper and pens for each table host to jot down ideas during the rounds.
- Snacks and beverages including gluten-free, nut-free, and dairy-free selections.
- Table host instructions—one per table.
- Handout of assessment summary and inclusion committee mission statement at each seat. You can send this out to each participant before the community conversation to save time.

Table Host Instructions

1. Welcome everyone.
2. Facilitate introductions. Keep it simple by asking people to only share their names, and no other information.
3. Remind people that they can write or doodle their ideas, discoveries, and deeper questions on their placemats.
4. Keep the conversation on track.
5. Remain at your table when it's time to switch groups, follow steps 1 through 4.
6. At the second round, share several insights from the previous group so the participants can link to these as well as use ideas from their previous groups.

Agenda

Introduction to the Community Conversation
Time: 10-15 minutes

- The facilitator welcomes everyone. With limited time, people can meet each other in their small groups, but there will not be time for everyone to introduce themselves.
- Frame the conversation. State why inclusion is important.
- Share information and background–include the assessment summary, the inclusion committee mission, and the purpose for the community conversation. Send this information out ahead of time, and provide a handout for reference by participants during the conversation. Information can also be presented in a short slide presentation.
- Outline the conversation process.

Small Group Rounds
Time: One hour

- Three small group rounds of twenty minutes each, during which participants discuss a question and brainstorm ideas.
- The same question will be discussed in rounds one and two. A new question will be discussed in round three.
- After each round, participants change tables to sit with different people.
- A placemat is provided at each seat to write down thoughts. Table hosts will take notes.

Large Group "Harvest"
Time: 45 minutes

While the facilitator guides the discussion, one of the organizers can write the ideas generated on flip chart pages posted around the room. Also have two people capture and record the "harvest" electronically. This is to ensure that everything is recorded.

- Share ideas, resources, and strategies. Table hosts share some of the ideas generated in the small groups, and participants add their ideas. 20 minutes.

- After harvesting the ideas, ask the large group to identify which ideas to integrate into the roadmap, or action plan. 20 minutes.

- Use this opportunity to issue a call to action. Ask participants to choose one thing that they will do as a result of the community conversation. The inclusion committee will create a list of people, how they would like to be involved, and follow up with each person.

- Collect the placemats and written notes. The inclusion committee will review these to see if there are other ideas that weren't captured.

- Thank everyone for participating in the community conversation and making it a success.

After the Community Conversation

The community conversation generates excitement and interest. Following up with the participants is a way to keep them engaged in inclusion. They will be eager to learn about what happens next, and some may want to be involved in various activities, such as developing the action plan, or working on the individual goals in the plan.

- The inclusion committee will organize the information

you recorded from the community conversation and email to the participants.

- The inclusion committee will use the ideas, resources, and strategies generated by the community conversation to help develop a formal action plan.

  Consider these factors when choosing priorities.
  - o Effectiveness in advancing belonging and inclusion.
  - o Impact on individuals with disabilities and mental health conditions, and those who love them.
  - o Urgent needs.
  - o Overall community awareness and engagement.

- Review the list you created and invite people to get involved in a specific activity, such as participating in developing the road map, or working with others to raise awareness.

- Share the results of the community conversation in a variety of ways, including an article in your weekly email, a sermon, staff meeting, newsletter, or video blog.

Now you're ready to develop your roadmap.

Food for Thought:
- What are some of the ways that the community conversation helped increase the interest in inclusion in your organization?
- What were some of the ideas generated that helped you think differently about belonging and inclusion?

Chapter 10

CREATE YOUR ROADMAP

Good intentions alone, not accompanied by action, are without value. The main thing is the action, for this is what makes the intention so profound.

— Rabbi Yaakov Yitzchak of Przysucha,
quoted in *Itturei Torah, Sh'mot* 10:24[1]

We all have good intentions to be the kind of inclusive community where people with disabilities and mental health conditions feel that they belong. But in order to realize those good intentions, you must have a plan.

Good intentions unsupported by action are wishes.

Convene the inclusion committee to design the roadmap for a more inclusive organization. Some inclusion committees schedule a two-hour meeting to complete these steps. Depending on how your committee operates, you can also schedule two shorter meetings, or assign a sub-group to each goal.

This is the process.

- Develop one or more goals for each priority.
- Choose the actions necessary to achieve the goals.
- Create a timeline to achieve the overall goal.
- Break goals into tasks, anticipated due dates, people assigned to complete each task, and actual completion date.
- Include people outside of the inclusion committee to partner with you.

Develop Goals for Each Priority

- Once you have set two to three priorities, you can write the goals for each. Use the goal setting form in this chapter or in the **Companion Workbook** to formalize your plan.
- Break the goal down into tasks, due date, and the person responsible. Fill in the date when each task is completed.

Include Partners in Your Goals

Make a list of people, committees, and departments within your organization who you can ask to partner with the inclusion committee. Include clergy, lay leaders, committee chairs, employees, and others. Look for resources in your community, such as disability organizations, social services agencies, and the national, regional, and local disability initiatives of your religious affiliation.

Share the Roadmap

Summarize each of the goal sheets. This provides the big picture view of the priorities and goals and becomes the formal inclusion plan. Share it with the administration, clergy, board, and department heads and get everyone committed to the Structure of Inclusion.

Sample Roadmap

A blank goal setting form is on page 148 and in the **Companion Workbook.** Following are examples of goals and action plans. This faith community decided that they would focus on two priorities—communication and raising awareness. The inclusion committee felt that these priorities would address the urgency around inclusion, have an impact on individuals with disabilities and mental health conditions and their loved ones, and engage and educate the whole community.

Goal Setting

Priority Addressed:			
GOAL:			
Today's Date: Date to Achieve Goal:		Date Completed:	
Tasks	**Due Date**	**Person(s) Responsible**	**Date Completed**
Comments:			

Priority Addressed: Communication

GOAL: To establish protocol for accommodations requests, signage, and dissemination of information about inclusion.

Today's Date: **Date to Achieve Goal:**   **Date Completed:**

Tasks	Due Date	Person(s) Responsible	Date Completed
Work with administration to include both inclusion and accommodation statements to appear in all written and electronic forms of communication.	2 months		
Develop procedures to respond to accommodation requests: who to contact; what questions to ask; what accommodations are currently available.	3 months		
Evaluate all signage—Are directional signs clear? Do they direct people to unobstructed routes? Are signs printed with contrasting backgrounds and text? Are signs easily seen by anyone using a wheelchair? Are signs in Braille?	2 months		
Determine how we communicate available resources and accommodations in information handbooks, service handouts, events, and programs.	2 months		
Comments:			

Priority Addressed: Raise Awareness GOAL: Educate the community as a whole about belonging and inclusion. Today's Date: Date to Achieve Goal: Date Completed:			
Tasks	Due Date	Person(s) Responsible	Date Completed
Appoint a task force to consider a month, week, or day to raise awareness. Get feedback from inclusion organization leadership on how to proceed.	3 months		
Assign a task force to plan and implement the raising awareness initiative.	8-9 months		
Talk to the usher committee chair about training ushers to support people with disabilities.	2 months		
Research what other faith communities have done to raise awareness, e.g. screen films, start a book club, host a speaker or panel on disability and mental health inclusion.	4 months		
Comments:			

Keep the Roadmap Current

Review your roadmap at all inclusion committee meetings. Track progress, discuss obstacles, and regularly revise goals or steps. Adapt any changes to the plan. Be sure to check off all the steps you make. Email short updates to the community conversation participants, clergy, executive director, and the board.

Before you know it, you will be celebrating the one-year anniversary of your community conversation. Schedule a review meeting of the inclusion committee and invite others who have expressed an interest in joining the committee. Discuss these questions and complete the Annual Review form in the **Companion Workbook.**

- Was this goal accomplished?
- What was effective in accomplishing this goal?
- How do you know this goal was accomplished?
- What changed as a result of achieving this goal?
- What didn't work toward accomplishing this goal?
- If the goal was not achieved, explain why.
- Should this goal be carried over to the next year?
- If so, what tasks should be added?

Review the remaining priorities from the community conversation. Identify which ones to work on and revise your goals.

Year two of your journey is about to begin.

Food for Thought:
- How does having an action plan make a difference in how you approach inclusion?
- What opportunities do you have now for recruiting more people from your organization to work on your inclusion initiative?

Chapter 11

PRACTICAL IDEAS AND EFFECTIVE STRATEGIES FOR INCLUSIVE ORGANIZATIONS

Everything has an appointed season, and there is a time for every matter under the heavens.

— Ecclesiastes 3:1

No One Does This Alone

You are ready to set your plan into motion. Think of your organization as a large tapestry, unique in design, color, and thread. Inclusion is woven into the entire tapestry and is part of every program, activity, and service you offer. As you read this chapter, look for ways you can incorporate these practical ideas into your organization.

- Report the summary of findings and the results of the community conversation to the governing board. Periodically give updates to the board in writing, or in a five-minute presentation at a meeting. Remember, board members can change from year to year—so it's appropriate to give new members a short orientation about inclusion.

- Stress the board members' responsibility to welcome everyone in the Spirit of Belonging.

- Invite committee chairs to an informational meeting to share the assessment summary and the action plan. Discuss how the inclusion committee can partner with them to advance inclusion. For example, if one of the goals is to increase participation of people with disabilities in worship services, partner with the appropriate committee to explore this issue together.

- Partner with another committee to collaborate on an educational program or host a potluck dinner or "Lunch and Learn."

- Maintain communication with the professional staff, board members, and committee chairs about your progress. Invite their support and expertise as you work your action plan.

- Be certain to *model* inclusion in your words and your actions.

- Create an endowment fund to provide for accessibility and inclusion needs.

- Let the entire organization in on what you are accomplishing. Publicize the work you are doing. Continue to ask for volunteers.

Review Your Organization's Mission Statement

Review your organization's mission statement through an inclusion lens. Does it accurately reflect the concept of belonging and your philosophy of inclusion? If not, suggest that the board change the mission statement.

Mission statements are meant to be adapted as organizations mature. Refer to Chapter 7, "Getting Started," for examples of mission statements and steps to develop them.

Communicate the Spirit of Belonging in Membership Information and Applications

Create a statement that articulates the importance of belonging and inclusion. Statements such as the ones that follow can be powerful invitations to someone who is seeking a place to belong.

- We believe that inclusion is more than a cherished value—it is a way of life in our community.
- We believe that people come to our congregation seeking to belong, to contribute, and to flourish.
- We believe in building relationships and working together to achieve a sense of belonging.
- We believe our community is richer when people participate together, with the understanding that each one of us is created in God's image.

Include this question on all applications.
"What accommodations, if any, would be helpful to you to participate?"

The Role of Clergy

Clergy can show their support for inclusion by endorsing the formation of an inclusion committee, identifying lay leaders, and advising them. They can attend inclusion committee meetings or appoint a representative from the professional staff, give sermons, and provide theological and spiritual context.

Here are ideas to create open communication between clergy and the inclusion committee.

- Meet with clergy to discuss why you want to pursue inclusion in your congregation. Ask for their support.
- Ask what role they see taking in this mission. Some

congregations choose to designate a member of the clergy as the liaison to the inclusion committee.

- Invite a member of the clergy to come to your first inclusion committee meeting to offer a blessing, and speak about inclusion. Offer thanks for supporting the committee.
- Include clergy in all committee updates and meeting minutes.
- Interview clergy in the assessment process and invite them to the community conversation.
- Discuss how the inclusion committee can serve as a resource to clergy.
- Help build community—address issues together such as transportation, life-cycle preparation, confirmation, family support, childcare, and sign language interpretation.
- Finally, ask your clergy "What can we do together to become more inclusive?

Inclusion and Organizational Committees

Inclusion committee members can sit on other committees to provide insights and strategies to help foster inclusion in other areas of ministry, events, and activities.

Invite a member from each committee to sit on the inclusion committee or attend a meeting. Ask that they report back to their own committee.

Consider offering a presentation or short training to other committees at their meetings. The inclusion committee can lead the way in teaching others to look for opportunities to include and support people with disabilities and mental health conditions.

The inclusion committee should not be the only volunteer experience available to people with disabilities. People like to volunteer in their own areas of interest and concern. By having members with a disability sit on other committees, they can help infuse the entire community with the spirit of belonging.

Inclusion in Leadership and Volunteer Opportunities

In every organization, people with diverse skills and talents are called upon to lead. They serve as board members, committee chairs and members, staff members, and volunteers. A person's ability to lead and contribute should be based on their skills, talents, interests, and abilities to serve the organization and not on the disability.

Volunteering is an opportunity for people to give back to the community, and become even more involved.

Funding Inclusion

Many houses of worship and other religious organizations were built well before 1990 when the Americans with Disabilities Act (ADA) became law. The ADA provides regulations for access to buildings and grounds. Religious organizations generally are not covered under the ADA. However, religious organizations should use the ADA as a guide for renovations and new construction. Any capital campaigns should include a budget for accessibility.

The ADA provides standards for universal design or inclusive design of buildings and environments in order to provide access for all people, regardless of disability, age, or other factors. For example, a ramp provides access to people who use mobility devices, wheelchairs, and walkers, as well as those who have difficulty breathing, and parents who use strollers All of them depend on having access to both exterior and interior spaces.

There are many no-cost and low-cost modifications that enable people to participate in community life. Some simple accommodations, such as providing large print copies of materials, and changing the location of meetings and programs to accessible spaces or an off-site facility, may require a little extra effort, but they are not necessarily expensive.

Budgeting for Inclusion

There are a number of ways to fund inclusion in your organization. Consider these options as you develop an ongoing plan to put inclusion on your fiscal map.

Audit Inclusion Costs

Review the costs you have incurred over the last three budget cycles to determine what percentage of the annual budget has been spent on inclusion. A budget audit shows the types of projects and accommodations that were funded, the area in which they were incurred, and whether they were regular expenditures or one-time expenses. Specify what the expenditures were in the following categories:

- Religious education
- Life-cycle event education and preparation
- Structural modifications and accommodations—including ramps, automatic door openers, lighting, accessible parking, etc.
- Communications devices—audio loops, large print and Braille prayer books, sign language interpreters, Communication Access Real Time Translation (CART)
- Adult education
- Worship
- Youth groups
- Camp
- Social and cultural activities

- Accommodations for staff members with disabilities

After reviewing the last two or three budget cycles, answer the following questions. Include your findings in a report to the finance committee and in all subsequent budget discussions.

1. How were funding requests for inclusion handled in the past?
2. Which requests were funded? What amount was requested? What amount was funded? If not fully funded, why not?
3. Which requests were not funded?
4. Why were these requests not funded?
5. What plans are in place to address the requests that were not funded or fully funded—such as fund them in a later fiscal year, scale them back, determine their necessity, etc.?
6. What percentage of the total inclusion budget was allocated to each area?
7. What percentage came from the general operating budget?
8. Does the general operating budget have a standard allocation for inclusion, or is inclusion part of the annual budgeting process?
9. What percentage came from additional fundraising?
10. Will additional fundraising opportunities be repeated?
11. What percentage came from designated funds?
12. Do those designated funds still have money in them? Can the funds be replenished?
13. Has anyone in the organization been approached to start an endowment fund for inclusion? If so, what was the result? If not, why not?

Line-Item Strategy

Because inclusion involves every program and project in your organization, it is essential to proactively incorporate an accommodation line item into each departmental and administrative budget, as well as every project. This is a reliable way to ensure resources are available. By following this process, you are ensuring that inclusion needs are considered each time programming decisions are made.

Review the budget audit data to determine the percentage of the past three annual budgets spent on inclusion-related costs. As you develop a new annual budget, this information will help allocate funds for inclusion.

Long-range planning initiatives should address costlier expenditures needed for the building and grounds so future funding is secured. Your evaluation and assessment of the building and grounds will help you prioritize modifications to the structure.

Designated Funds

Designated funds are established with the intent they will provide financial resources for specific needs in your organization. The clergy or the executive director might be able to identify particular areas of need for which they have sought funds in the past. You can also brainstorm with them to develop a list of potential fund opportunities.

Types of designated funds:

- General inclusion
- Sign language interpreters
- Religious special education
- Adaptive technology and special equipment
- Transportation

- Classroom/camp advocates or assistants

Be sure the title of the fund indicates that it provides funds to support people with disabilities or mental health conditions.

Foundations and Grants

Research if there are any philanthropic foundations that provide grants to faith-based organizations which support participation by people with disabilities and mental health conditions.

Fundraising

Fundraising for inclusion can be very simple. Here are some suggestions:

- Dedicate a dollar amount to be allocated from the school or camp registration fees to support inclusion.
- If your organization sends out billing statements, ask people to designate an additional contribution for inclusion.
- Collaborate with the arts committee to raise funds at a community "Arts for Inclusion" event, such as a concert, theatre performance, guest speaker, or an art exhibit. The committees can share in the proceeds from the event.
- Designate a special fundraiser to benefit a particular need. For example, one congregation sold flowers each spring to raise money to purchase fidget toys to help students focus better in their classes.
- When you have a specific item that requires funding, publicize it in your bulletins, emails, and all other

communications. Ask for funding!

Practical No-Cost and Low-Cost Accommodations

Besides budgeting and raising money for inclusion, your organization can take immediate steps that are simple to implement.

- Inform people that accessible parking spaces are *only* for individuals who have an accessible parking tag hanging on the mirror of the vehicles, or those who have a disability license plate. Besides posting signage, include this information in all communications. Enforce compliance.
- Use the universal blue-and-white accessibility symbol to clearly mark accessible entrances.
- Welcome everyone by positioning greeters at building entrances to open doors, give directions, and offer assistance.
- Use portable ramps if you do not have permanent ones to the building or pulpit. Ask your state ADA office to help you determine the rise required for the ramp. Some buildings and outside entrances are not long enough to use them without a steep rise.
- After a snowstorm, first shovel the snow and remove ice on all accessible routes. If accessible routes are cleared first, everyone can use them. Maintain accessible pathways into and out of the building.
- Reserve seating that's directly in front of sign language interpreters for deaf participants.
- Make sure all lighting is as bright as possible and provide magnifiers so people can see the printed materials.

- Use signage to direct people to accessible restrooms. If automatic door openers are not available, offer assistance opening the doors.
- Order a sufficient number of large print prayer books, hymnals, bibles, and other printed materials. If you create your own materials, such as prayer books and service handouts, have large-print copies available.
- Enhance the worship experience through art and photographs projected on a screen, or downloaded to a tablet or phone. Visual worship adds a new layer of understanding and engagement in prayer for many people and gives our hearts and minds another spiritual connection. Visual worship also appeals to the neurodiversity of worshippers in our congregations. You can find many excellent online resources to help you create the visual worship experience.
- Place paper cups and a wastebasket near drinking fountains to improve access for people who cannot reach the fountain.

Use Language That Shows Respect

The language a faith community uses to describe people with disabilities and mental health conditions demonstrates communal attitudes toward inclusion and belonging. We respect a person's humanity, not only through how we treat each other, but also through the language we use. Appropriate language reflects inherent respect and dignity.

Start with understanding the definition of "disability" and the outdated, but often still used term "handicap."

The ADA defines a person with a disability as a person who has a physical or mental impairment that substantially limits one or more major life activities. This includes people who have a record of such an impairment, even if they do not currently have a disability.

Some people may have more than one disability.

A *handicap* is a physical or attitudinal constraint that is imposed upon a person, regardless of whether he has a disability. A handicap puts a person at a disadvantage.

Example: Some people with disabilities use wheelchairs.

Example: Stairs, narrow doorways, and curbs are *handicaps* imposed upon people who use wheelchairs.

The most common use of "handicap" involves physical access. We use the blue-and-white wheelchair symbol to indicate accessible parking, entrances, and restrooms. We commonly refer to these as "handicap" parking, entrances, and restrooms. It is more accurate to use the term "accessible" to describe these accommodations.

Identifying Language

How do you refer to a person with a disability? Terms such as "handicapped" and "disabled" are throwbacks to earlier decades. Person First language is used to reframe how people with disabilities are regarded by putting the person before the disability. Examples of Person First language:

- Say that Sarah is a person with a disability rather than Sarah is disabled or handicapped.
- People with disabilities are involved in congregational leadership rather than disabled people are involved in congregational leadership.

However, the language we use to describe people with disabilities is not one-size-fits-all. I was talking with my friend about involving people with disabilities in our congregation.

Sharon, who has lived with a disability her whole life, said, "We have to support disabled people to be involved in the congregation." I shot back, "Sharon, we don't say 'disabled people' anymore. We say 'people with disabilities.'"

Sharon patiently replied, "What difference does it make? I'm a disabled person. I always have been and I always will be."

Sharon's identity as a disabled person is an example of Identity First language. The Association of University Centers on Disabilities (AUCD) notes that Identity First language "emphasizes that the disability plays a role in who the person is, and reinforces disability as a positive cultural identifier. Identity-first language is generally preferred by people in the autistic, Deaf, and blind communities."[1]

Language to Avoid Altogether

- Cripple/handicapped/handicap/invalid
- Victim/afflicted by/afflicted with
- Differently abled
- Normal—referring to non-disabled persons as "normal" insinuates that people with disabilities and mental health conditions are abnormal
- Deaf mute/deaf and dumb
- Birth defect
- Crazy/insane/mental/nuts
- Fits
- Slow/retarded
- Abnormal/deformed

Avoid euphemisms. Some organizations use the term "special needs" when referring to people with disabilities. Euphemisms can evoke pity and patronization, indicating people with disabilities require special care, special programs, or special services that separate them from the community. "Disability" is considered to be non-judgmental and factual. It currently is the preferred terminology and is a more authentic description without any judgment attached to it, positive or negative.

Avoid certain terms or phrases which diminish the humanity of a person. For example, when people say, "Put the wheelchair over there in the spot we reserved" they really mean, "We've reserved an accessible spot for a person who uses a wheelchair." The wheelchair is an accommodation that gives the user access to buildings and interior spaces like anyone else.

Avoid phrases such as "wheelchair bound," or "confined to a wheelchair." My friend Celia went everywhere using her wheelchair. She wasn't bound to her wheelchair. It gave her the freedom to live her life as she chose.

Language used to describe disability continues to evolve.

**Ask a person if they have a preference for how
they want to be identified.
Most likely, they will say, "Yes. Call me by my name!"**

Accessibility For Your Website

Do you know if your website and other electronic communications are accessible to people with disabilities? If not, it is time to update all electronic communication so that everyone has access to your digital content.

Web accessibility means that websites, tools, and technologies are designed and developed to provide equal access and opportunities for people with diverse abilities.[2] Web accessibility allows people with disabilities to understand, perceive, navigate, and interact on the internet.

Web accessibility encompasses all disabilities that affect access to the Web, including:

- Auditory
- Cognitive
- Neurological
- Physical
- Speech
- Visual

There are a number of aspects to designing for web accessibility. The W3C Web Accessibility Initiative (WAI) develops standards and support materials to help you understand and implement accessibility.[3]

Publicize Accessibility and Inclusion

Publicizing accessibility and inclusion makes a statement about your community values. Many congregations and faith-based organizations have architectural and communications accommodations—but they fail to publicize them on websites, bulletins, signage, in emails, and program handouts. Be sure to include an accommodation statement when you publicize an event on social media or in the press.

Printed Information

- Newsletters and annual reports
- Worship services handouts
- Event programs
- Membership packets
- Religious education packets

- Invitations to events
- Fundraising mailers
- All press releases, publicity, and articles in local, religious, and secular press
- Signs posted at entrances and other high-traffic areas directing people to accessible restrooms and elevators

Online Information

- Website main page
- Social media posts
- Electronic invitations to events, annual meetings, and services
- Organizational e-mails

Accessibility Statements and Accommodation Requests

Include an accessibility statement in *all* electronic and written publications, registration forms, and websites. An accessibility statement clearly states that your organization welcomes people with disabilities, including all services, classes, events, meetings, and programs. See Appendix B for further information and sample accessibility and accommodation statements.

Develop a Safety Plan

Every organization needs to develop a plan that includes the safety of people with disabilities.

These questions will help you think about individual safety in an emergency.

- Do you conduct regular fire and emergency drills that include the safety of people with disabilities?
- What is your plan for someone who cannot use the

stairwells to exit the building, hear emergency communications, or see where to go in an emergency?

- What is your plan for moving the person with mobility restrictions to the safest location possible (depending on the type of emergency)?
- How would you communicate the person's location to emergency personnel once they arrive on the scene?
- Do you have a buddy system in place so the person with mobility restrictions is not alone while waiting for the emergency evacuation?

Steps to Create a Safety Plan

1. Ask local law enforcement or emergency responders to conduct an audit of your building and offer suggestions on how to best evacuate people or shelter them in place.

2. Prepare an evacuation plan and share it with all staff members. Post this critical information on your website and at locations throughout the building so everyone has it.

3. Ask congregants, participants, clients, and co-workers with disabilities, including those with vision, hearing, and mobility disabilities, about their personal evacuation concerns and needs.

4. Train your staff and volunteers to assist people in emergency protocol. They are responsible for locating people in an emergency and providing assistance.

5. Practice emergency protocol in all areas of your organization. Schedule emergency drills when the building is in use for services, school, and all other events.

Although a drill will disrupt planned activities, should an emergency ever arise, participants will be prepared.

6. Test smoke detectors, public announcement systems, fire extinguishers, and flashlights to make sure they are always working. Make sure alternate alert systems are available for individuals with disabilities, especially for people with vision and hearing disabilities.

Food Policy

Many people have sensitivity to particular foods. Exposure to these allergens can cause severe and even life-threatening reactions. These suggestions should be included in an effective food policy.

- Restrict the kinds of food served or brought into the building. For example, many preschools do not allow peanut butter.
- Require that food is purchased from a grocery store or bakery.
- Require ingredients to be labeled for *all* food served.
- Require alternative gluten-free, dairy-free, and tree nut-free items

Scent-Free Policy

Many organizations have a scent-free policy so individuals with chemical sensitivities are not exposed to a significant health risk. Include a scent-free policy statement in your bulletin, newsletter, invitations, and tickets to events.

Sample Statement: Many individuals have extreme reactions to fragrances including perfume, cologne, aftershave, body lotions and creams, and hair products. Avoid wearing any of these products, as exposure to them may cause a severe allergic reaction in some individuals.

Event Planning

What is the next big event for your organization? An annual meeting, a fundraiser or gala, a speaker event, concert, or an ice cream social? Inclusion isn't an afterthought—it's a priority. Make all events inclusive from the beginning of the planning. The Event Planning Checklist in Appendix C and in the **Companion Workbook** will guide you through the entire process.

The Americans with Disabilities Act
A Moral Mandate for Faith Communities

Rabbi Lynne Landsberg was the Associate Director of the Religious Action Center of Reform Judaism (RAC) when she sustained a traumatic brain injury in a car accident. She said, "As Associate Director, the first major bill I worked on was the ADA. Little did I know that a decade later, the legislation would directly affect my life."

After many months of recovery and therapies following the accident, Rabbi Landsberg returned to the RAC as Senior Advisor on Disability Rights. The ADA now affected her directly.

Many religious groups tirelessly advocated for passage of the ADA. After the ADA passed, Rabbi Landsberg was surprised to learn that due to pressure from other religious groups, whatever their reasons, houses of worship were exempt from, and therefore, did not have to comply with significant portions of the ADA.

However, faith communities do have a moral mandate to follow the spirit of the ADA. See Appendix A to learn more about the ADA and your faith community.

Food for Thought:

- What specific steps in this chapter can you implement immediately?
- What are one or two long-range ideas that will further inclusion in your organization?

Chapter 12

EDUCATING YOUR COMMUNITY

And God created humans in God's image.

— Genesis 1:27

The journey from longing to belonging is not a solitary path for people with disabilities, mental health conditions, and those who love them. Educating the entire faith community about belonging and inclusion will help to eliminate attitudinal obstacles that marginalize people.

No matter how progressive an organization thinks it is, there is always room for improvement. A comprehensive approach to inclusion features two elements.

1. Support for the individual to ensure a sense of belonging and opportunities to participate in the life of the community
2. Education for the community about the values we hold and the responsibilities we have to maintain a culture of inclusion.

Raising Awareness Fuels Change

How important is educating your community about inclusion and belonging? Dr. Erik Carter and his team at the Vanderbilt University Kennedy Center asked parents of children with disabilities what faith communities could do to reduce obstacles to participation.[1] More than seventy percent of parents responded that congregation-wide disability awareness would be helpful. Researchers learned than just ten percent of the congregations offered this support. Obstacles caused by a lack of knowledge and outdated attitudes are often the reasons for lack of inclusion. Educating the entire community can go a long way in raising awareness and creating a culture that encourages active participation by all of its members.

Faith communities can begin to raise awareness by simply talking about disability inclusion in services, study sessions, staff meetings, and classrooms. With a wealth of religious, spiritual, and theological resources available to provide context, there is no shortage of ways to introduce religious and spiritual values.

Consider these questions when you launch your raising awareness campaign:

1. What is a disability? What is a mental health condition?
2. How do you know if a person has a disability or mental health condition?
3. Why would someone who has a disability or mental health condition be unable to participate?
4. What are some obstacles to inclusion and belonging?
5. Are there specific rituals that people with disabilities should not perform?
6. How are people with disabilities or mental health conditions mentioned in the Bible?
7. What percentage of people living in our community has disabilities? (Nearly twenty percent) Mental health conditions? (Twenty percent).[2]
8. How could this congregation/organization be more supportive so people with disabilities and mental health conditions can participate in all the activities we offer?
9. What needs to change in order to be a community where people feel they belong?
10. How has your thinking about disability changed over time? What do you think fostered this change?

Create a Raising Awareness Campaign

Convene a task force to manage a campaign to raise awareness. The task force could be a sub-group of the inclusion committee. If you don't have an inclusion committee yet, the task force may be the first step to starting one.

Brainstorm ideas about what you want people to know about inclusion. Some suggestions for raising awareness are to:

- Provide an overview of the Spirit of Belonging and the Structure of Inclusion.
- Explain the theological concept of inclusion and its implications.
- Show statistics about the number of people who live with disabilities or mental health conditions.
- Demonstrate ways your organization is working to be more inclusive and welcoming.
- Describe the role each person can play.

Decide on the scope of your campaign. Will you have a Sabbath of Inclusion, an educational program, or a week or month of programming? Do you want to educate the entire community or focus only on particular groups?

Determine how to raise awareness:

- Give a sermon on inclusion.
- Invite people with disabilities, mental health conditions, and their families to participate in the service, lead prayers, or give a talk.
- Host a multisensory worship service.
- Start each service with the opportunity for congregants to turn to their neighbors and introduce themselves. Make sure every person has someone with whom to share a greeting.

- Schedule a Lunch and Learn to explore Bible commentary on disability and inclusion.
- Schedule a movie night. Choose from a variety of full-length and short films about people who live with a disability or mental health condition.
- Host a book discussion about an autobiography or a novel depicting life with a disability or mental health condition.
- Host a panel discussion about what it means to belong to a faith community. Panelists can include clergy, people with disabilities and mental health conditions, and family members.
- Have a board discussion on how lay leaders can advance inclusion.
- Host a congregational dinner to launch a week or month-long awareness campaign.
- Invite a speaker from a local disability service agency to talk about their work.
- Invite a speaker from a disability or social service organization to lead a parent discussion about common concerns. Offer childcare.
- Provide curriculum for your preschool and congregational school about religious values and inclusion.
- Read books and stories written about children with a diverse range of abilities and strengths.

Collaborate with Faith Community and Secular Organizations

Faith community organizations can partner with others to host community-wide conferences. Organizations can share planning, resources and costs to reach a wider audience. Consider including local disability organizations, such as The Arc, Autism Society, or National Alliance on Mental Illness (NAMI) to help with planning and marketing to a wide audience.

Community-wide events can include:

- Resource fair with disability organizations, parent training centers, and authors of books on disabilities, mental health conditions, parenting, or autobiographies.
- Keynote speaker and book signing.
- Workshops on a wide range of topics.
- Screenings of short or feature films followed by a discussion.
- Music, theatre or dance performances, and art exhibits by people who have disabilities or mental health conditions.

Before you choose a date and venue for your community conference, meet with potential partners and discuss how each organization can contribute to the conference in any of the following ways:

- Financial contribution: Defray costs of speakers, venue, rentals of ramps, technical equipment, tables, and chairs, as needed, and food. Ask for in-kind contributions, e.g. conference space, printing, equipment rentals, food.
- Finances: Disperse funds to speakers, venue, food, and equipment vendors.
- Marketing and promotion: Create social media buzz, emails, and press releases to promote the event including speakers, workshops, and registration information.
- Speakers: Maintain contact with keynote speakers and workshop presenters, schedule sessions, gather and print handouts.

- Attendees: Manage on-line and paper registrations, conference fees–if any, disability accommodations, food requests, conference evaluations.
- Resource Fair vendors: Market to potential vendors, collect registrations and fees, assign table locations.
- Food vendors: Choose menus, determine food costs, handle special food requests, provide final count.
- Workshops: Assign room locations, check that microphones and equipment are working in the assigned rooms, distribute handouts to workshops, set up seating arrangements, and provide directional signage.
- Coordinate the set-up and tear down of conference space.

Food for Thought:
- What did your organization do in the past to raise awareness?
- What did you learn from this chapter that you would like to explore with your organization?

Chapter 13

INCLUSIVE WORSHIP EXPERIENCES

*"The house of worship represents one place where the barriers fall
and we all stand equal before God."*
– Rabbi Harold Kushner[1]

Nearly twenty percent of people in the United States have a disability. Twenty percent of people have a mental health diagnosis.[2] Do you know how many of them are worshipping with your congregation or are longing to be there?

Worship is a main point of entry into congregational life and is no less significant for someone who lives with a disability. Belonging starts in your sanctuary.

Prayer spaces provide people with disabilities and mental health conditions a safe and nurturing environment to explore their spiritual, religious, and communal needs and aspirations. Being in a community of worshippers—praying together, hearing scripture read and interpreted, celebrating life-cycle events, finding comfort for their losses, and joining others for fellowship and food—all contribute to the Spirit of Belonging.

Within the confines of a sanctuary each of us is unique. The same prayers can mean something different to the person sitting right next to you. Our beliefs, faith, and relationship with God are also personal and unique. We manifest our spiritual selves from the heart, the head, the soul, and the body. There is no one "right" way to worship.

Barbara Newman, author of *Accessible Gospel, Inclusive Worship*[3] in a personal communication said, "When the church, synagogue, or mosque says, 'We don't have those people here,' and if it's true that God hand-knit each person, and you just sent someone away, who loses? The person doesn't have access to the richness of the community. The community also loses because it doesn't have access to the person that God put together in this way."

Barbara continued, "Worship is where everyone can participate. Some people are easy to get to know. With some people you have to dig further. Too often we ask the wrong question, 'What can't this person do?' The right question to ask is, 'What can this person do?'"

Prayer rituals carry memories, reminding us of parents, grandparents, friends, and others upon whose shoulders we stand. Personal history nuances the words on the page and transforms them in our hearts. It's not just prayer that can be deeply personal; it is *all* that faith, spirituality, religion, and community encompass.

Elaine Hall is the parent of an autistic son, author of *Now I See the Moon,*[4] and creator of *Inclusion from WithIn (I Win)*, a program for faith-based communities. Elaine, who was profiled in the HBO film *Autism: The Musical,* uses "reverse inclusion." She said, "Separating individuals with disabilities from the rest of the congregation does a disservice to everyone. 'Reverse inclusion' brings typically developing peers into the world of those with a disability." This creates a neurodiverse community where everyone belongs. Elaine uses small groups to teach the nuances of worship services so individuals of all abilities can then participate in communal worship experiences.

Elaine invited me to attend a service that was co-led by young adults on the autistic spectrum. Her son Neal, who is non-speaking, wrote a moving sermon about inclusion that was read by a congregant. Jessica, a young woman with a beautiful voice, inspired the congregation as she chanted a prayer. Elaine told me that Neal, Jessica, and the others who led services felt a sense of belonging and connection. She added, "Many congregants wrote emails saying that this service was one of the most meaningful one they had ever attended."

Because faith communities have begun to welcome people with disabilities and mental health conditions, we must consider what it means to engage in the congregation's rituals of prayer and worship. Faith communities may unintentionally shut people out from the essential practice of communal worship. Common myths include thinking that prayer is too intellectual, too esoteric, or too involved for people with disabilities to understand. Some well-meaning congregations create a separate service that distances people from the rest of the community.

Worship Etiquette

When someone comes to services for the first time, they may not be familiar with the congregational culture and rituals. Will they know which prayer book to use, which prayers are read and which are sung, or when to stand, sit, or kneel?

In a welcoming and inclusive congregation, the Spirit of Belonging is exemplified by how members interact with people who are unfamiliar with the service.

Examine your rituals to see how they might restrict people from participating in worship. You may need to alter a ritual to make it accessible. Such accommodations may not alter the intent, and in fact, may interject new meaning into a ritual.

For example, many faith traditions require people to stand at particular times during the service. Some congregations, recognizing that there are worshippers who may not physically stand, have adapted their "stand" language. They have created their own language, such as "Please stand as you are able," or "Please rise in body and in spirit." To introduce this adapted ritual to the congregation, it is helpful to explain the purpose for the change in language.

There are many variations of "stand" language and you may want to explore different ways to approach what to say. Rabbi David Locketz, of Bet Shalom Congregation in Minneapolis, began the Yom Kippur service with this comment on "stand" language. He said, "Throughout our service, when our liturgy calls for it, I will be inviting you to rise and stand together as a congregation. I also recognize that may be a difficulty for some people. If you are not able to rise when the liturgy calls for it, don't fret. Sit comfortably. If you can stand up, I invite you to when the time comes. But whether you are sitting or standing, your prayers will be accepted the same. May we together be carried to the great heights that our rituals are intended to take us to."

Ushers Make the First Impression

The congregation's ushers were meeting and greeting people with disabilities more frequently. In the true Spirit of Belonging, the ushers wanted all people, congregants and guests, to experience how friendly and welcoming the community could be.

The ushers noticed that they didn't always know how to approach someone with a disability. One usher didn't realize he was speaking loudly to a teenage girl who used a wheelchair until she gently told him that her hearing was just fine. Another usher couldn't find the assistive listening device a visitor was promised after he called the church office to let them know he needed this accommodation. When a young adult was visiting the congregation for the first time, the ushers didn't know what to do when he began making loud noises during a hymn. When other worshippers turned and cast disapproving looks at him, the ushers asked his caregiver to take him out of the sanctuary.

It was challenging to meet everyone's needs and the ushers

needed guidance. The inclusion committee agreed to work with the ushers.

Ushers are often the first point of contact in houses of worship. A short training session on etiquette and how to make someone feel welcome can ease uncertainty. Training raises awareness and offers the opportunity to discuss how to manage new situations. Use the following outline for training ushers and others in your organization who are in a position to welcome and greet people. The inclusion committee can facilitate the training, which takes approximately 30 minutes.

Usher Training

Welcome to usher training. We're here to explore how ushers can help provide a comfortable and inclusive worship experience for people with disabilities:

- Ushers are often the first point of contact in our congregation. Training will help you make the experience a positive one for all congregants and visitors.
- Nearly twenty percent of the population has a disability. You will meet people with disabilities in your role as an usher.
- In our desire to be helpful and welcoming, we often make assumptions about what a person needs. This training will help you feel more comfortable addressing individual needs.
- Learn what accommodations we provide, and how to locate and use them.

Basic Disability Awareness

- We believe each person is a unique individual, created in the Divine Image.
- Belonging to this community is important to people. Overcoming barriers and making accommodations for people to participate is a community value.
- We treat people as *they* want to be treated—with respect, dignity, and honor.
- Each person has gifts, strengths, contributions, and needs. All are welcome here.
- Disability is not a reason to exclude or segregate people from any of the activities and offerings of this community.
- Some disabilities are visible, such as cerebral palsy or Down syndrome.
- Some disabilities are not apparent, such as autism or learning disabilities.
- Disability can affect a person's life from birth, or can be acquired during one's lifetime.
- The rule of thumb: Just Ask! If you're uncertain about what to do, ask the person with a disability what they need in order to participate.
- Even when you think you know what accommodations someone needs, ask them first.
- If someone uses a wheelchair or is a person of short stature, greet them at their eye level.
- Use language that is respectful. Review "Use Language That Shows Respect" on page 163.
- Some people who do not speak communicate using sounds or physical movement. Look directly at the individual and ask them—not their caregiver, if there is

something you can help with.

Before the Service

- Post one of the ushers at building entrances to greet people and give directions.
- Place large print copies of the service handout at all sanctuary/chapel entrances.
- Make sure assistive listening devices are available and working.
- If a sign language interpreter will be present, reserve seats in the front row for people using interpretive services and their companions. Provide chairs for the interpreters.
- Remove objects that block doorways and automatic doors.
- Identify the most direct and barrier-free ways to access the social hall, restrooms, and building exits.
- Know where large-print and Braille prayer books, hymnals, and bibles, stands to hold prayer books, congregation-owned wheelchairs, walkers, canes, magnifying glasses or readers, accessible restrooms and a designated quiet room are located.
- Reserve several seats around the sanctuary so people who use wheelchairs can sit with their companions. Create "reserved" signs to place on the floor if you remove chairs to accommodate people who use wheelchairs.
- Place a portable coat rack near accessible entrances and elevators.
- Put paper cups and a wastebasket adjacent to drinking fountains.

Sanctuary Tours

Remember the very first time you entered your house of worship? Did you know where to go? Did you know where to sit? Were you curious about the different items used in the service? Some people may not feel comfortable in a new environment. When you meet someone new to your congregation and learn about their interests and how they want to participate, offer a tour of the sanctuary and other spaces.

Explore the Sanctuary or Chapel

Approach the tour of the sanctuary as if you have never been there before.

- Where do you like to sit? Let people experiment with sitting in different locations.
- If someone uses a wheelchair, show them the accessible sections and let them try out different spots.
- If your congregation keeps worship materials in the pews, show them to people giving a brief description of what they are, and when they're used.
- If your congregation keeps worship materials separate from the pews, show people where to find them. Do they pick them off the shelf or does someone hand them out?
- Explain the process for going up for communion or a blessing.

Create a Visual Service Schedule

- A visual schedule provides picture cues rather than language cues to process and retrieve information. Visual schedules show the sequence of activities in the service. A visual schedule can be as simple as drawing symbols or finding images that represent each part of the service.

- You can also create a visual prayer book using subscription online resources which offer many simple and colorful figures of people, religious images, and symbols. However you create your visual service schedule, put the images in order, add the name of the prayer or part of the service, and print. Laminate the printed sheets so they are durable and put them in a binder.
- Be sure to make several copies and have them available at all services. Creating a visual schedule could be a meaningful project for students in your school.

Explore the Pulpit
- Show people how to access the pulpit.
- Spend a few moments sitting on the pulpit and examining the sanctuary from this vantage point.
- Explore ritual items associated with each prayer or part of the service. See and feel items used in services including Torah scrolls, reading pointers, chalices, communion, and *Kiddush* cups, baptismal font, etc. Describe how each item is used.
- Stand or sit at the altar, podium, or reading desk.
- Speak into the microphone.

Support Participation in Worship Services
The Spirit of Belonging extends beyond sitting in the pews. Participating and contributing to the congregation includes being a part of the worship service. When you have an opportunity for congregants to lead part of the service or participate in a particular ritual, remember to include people with disabilities and mental health conditions. Your invitation to participate in services could

be the answer to someone's prayers.

Turn Separate Services into Communal Services

One of the benefits of congregational life is being part of the community. Through communal worship, we are bound together in the public act of praising God and reflecting on our own spiritual connection. Congregations have worship decorum that may not tolerate distracting behavior, such as fidgeting, making vocalizations during the service, or freely walking about the sanctuary. Some congregations require that all worshippers stand when prompted, resulting in discomfort for people who are unable. We need to expand our definition and acceptance for more inclusive ways to worship God.

Challenging assumptions about the ability of people to participate in congregational worship can be awakening! Congregations sometimes assume that worship in the main service is too "intellectual" or complex for someone with a disability. In an effort to provide access to worship, some congregations create separate services that have been shortened, or use storytelling and song as devices to worship and preach. I have seen some of these services referred to as "inclusion" services even though only people with disabilities and caregivers are invited to attend.

Because separate services are designed to meet the diverse preferences and needs of worshipers they are often creative and engaging. People are allowed to stand, sit, move around, and have the freedom to express themselves in unique ways. These services often incorporate stories, movement, song, and musical instruments such as shakers and tambourines for people to use. Some congregations place a table of snacks and beverages in the back of the sanctuary.

What I love about these services is that they show there are many ways to worship and belong. Instead of limiting participation to a specific demographic of the community, these services should be open to all who wish to experience other ways to worship in community.

If you hold a separate service for people with disabilities, invite all congregants to attend this service. This is one way to be a community where all people belong.

We've seen and heard of people who have been asked to leave services because they are "disruptive" to some worshippers. Vocalization may be a form of communication and prayer for people who do not speak. An inclusive service doesn't silence people just because they pray differently. Every service should celebrate the unique ways people pray and connect with God.

A Prayer for All People to Belong

One practical way to highlight belonging and inclusion is to add a prayer to your service that opens hearts and minds to appreciate the unique value of each person. One of my favorite prayers can be offered in any faith tradition. Written by the Reverend Kate Chips, this following prayer was adapted by a pioneer in faith community inclusion, Ginny Thornburgh. It was published in *That All May Worship: An Interfaith Welcome to People with Disabilities*.[5] May you be blessed as you go on your journey of belonging and inclusion for all people.

An Interfaith Litany for Wholeness

(Written by the Reverend Kate Chips and adapted by Ginny Thornburgh)

Leader: Let us pray for all of God's people.

For people who are blind and cannot see, and for those who can see but are blind to the people around them.

Response: *God, in your mercy, help us touch each other.*

Leader: For people who move slowly because of accident, illness or disability, and for those who move too fast to be aware of the world in which they live.

Response: *God, in your mercy, help us work together.*

Leader: For people who are deaf and cannot hear, and for those who can hear but ignore the cries of others.

Response: *God, in your mercy, help us respond to each other.*

Leader: For people who learn slowly, for people who learn in different ways, and for people who learn quickly and easily but often choose ignorance.

Response: *God, in your mercy, help us to grow in your wisdom.*

Leader: For families, friends and caregivers who serve people with disabilities, and for those who feel awkward in their presence.

Response: *God, in your mercy, help us see each other with your eyes.*

Leader: For people who feel isolated by their disabilities, and for people who contribute to that sense of isolation.

Response: *God, in your mercy, change our lives.*

Leader: For all people in your creation that we may learn to respect each other, and learn how to live together in peace.

Response: *God, in your mercy, bind us together.*

All: Amen

Food for Thought:
- What can you do to change how you invite, encourage, and support people with disabilities and mental health conditions to be part of your services?
- What are the obstacles to people being able to worship in personally meaningful ways?

Chapter 14

SOCIAL INCLUSION AND BELONGING

Hillel said, "Do not separate yourself from the community."
—*Pirke Avot* (The Ethics of Our Fathers) 2:4

People join faith communities for a variety of reasons. Parents want their children to attend a religious school or camp. People look for a community of comfort when a loved one dies, where they can reflect on life and loss, and most importantly, feel they are not alone. Some people seek a congregation that reflects their preferences for prayer, practice, worship, and theology. Others want to study religious texts, volunteer, and find friends who share common interests. Perhaps people want to receive faith-based social services or participate in a community center. Whatever the reasons, faith communities fill many needs. Belonging is the foundation on which these needs are met.

Obstacles to Social Inclusion

Have you ever been to a gathering where you do not know anyone? You enter the space looking for a friendly face. Everybody seems to know someone. People hug and talk to each other. They are having fun!

Everyone seems to know what to do—except you.

No one even looks your way. No one greets you or asks your name. Maybe people here aren't ignoring you on purpose. But the result is the same. It's as if *you are invisible.*

Just one experience of social isolation may be enough to keep someone from ever returning, no matter how important being part of the community is to them.

Even as your faith community may feel welcoming to you, to someone who is new or returning after an illness, it may feel daunting, cold, and complex. Think about your own experiences. How do you feel valued and respected? Do people smile at you and greet you, ask how you are, and wait for an answer? Do others know your name?

Social inclusion does not just happen. What seems easy to some people might be terrifying to another.

Think about ways you can personally help someone feel included in social situations. Just these simple acts can make the difference between feeling invisible and knowing you are valued.

- Extend an invitation to sit together.
- Introduce them to your friends and include them in the conversation.
- Offer to show them around.
- Begin a conversation with them! Belonging, anyone?
- Social inclusion is making people feel valued and recognized. The feeling we get when someone shows us around, asks about us, shares something about themselves—that's the feeling of belonging.

Food for Thought:

- Discuss the opportunities for people to be more involved in the social fabric of your organization, and how to engage them.
- What are some ways to raise awareness about social inclusion and belonging in your organization so everyone feels empowered to reach out to others?

Chapter 15

INCLUDING THE YOUNGEST— EARLY CHILDHOOD EDUCATION

"This child opened a door for them that leads, and continues to lead, them to God's infinite palaces that they did not even know existed."[1]
— Rabbi Abraham Twerski, MD
and Ursula Schwartz, PhD

Early childhood education is a significant point of entry into the community for children with disabilities and those who love them. A religious preschool instills faith, values, traditions, and rituals, and develops skills that prepare young children for kindergarten and beyond. Preschool education also creates a natural community of peers as children begin friendships that go beyond the classroom. This chapter provides tools to understand how early childhood education can support a young child who may be experiencing developmental delays or who has a disability diagnosis.

Many parents look to their faith-community preschools to begin religious training and to integrate their children socially with their peers. The importance that parents place on a religious preschool creates a sacred responsibility for early childhood educators to teach each child according to their learning needs.

Preschool inclusion has many positive outcomes. Participation in inclusive settings impacts the experiences of children with disabilities and their peers without disabilities. It positively affects the attitudes and beliefs of children with typical development, as well as increases their knowledge of differences. Children with disabilities typically engage in social interaction less often and are at a higher risk for peer rejection than their non-disabled peers. Preschool encourages a natural community for all children where they learn to accept each other.

The Role of Early Childhood Education Providers

In the preschool educational setting, developmental differences may or may not be significant. Schools can develop a protocol that outlines specific procedures for teachers and administrators to follow when a classroom teacher has a concern about a child's development. All teacher concerns must be raised with the school director or administrator, and then documented.

Early childhood is frequently a time when developmental differences are noticed. It is *never appropriate* to diagnose a child, or suggest to a parent that their child may have a disability. Diagnosis is the purview of professionals who are trained and qualified to evaluate young children, and should do so only after a comprehensive assessment is performed.

Early Childhood Special Education

If a child is found to have a disability under the federal Individuals with Disabilities Education Act (IDEA), they qualify to receive special education services. These services are provided through their home school district's early childhood special education program. Depending on the child's needs, they may spend some of each day or week in a special education setting in order to receive the appropriate services.

Parents as School Partners

Parents whose children have developmental differences or disability diagnoses may feel particularly vulnerable. They are navigating unfamiliar territory that brings them into contact with professionals who seem to be taking control of their child's life. Medical providers, special educators, and social workers may be involved as parents seek to understand their child's needs—and what a diagnosis means to the child and their family.

It is so important for the preschool to have an open line of communication with parents. Parents of children with disabilities have the same goals and dreams of inclusion in their faith community for their children as all other parents.

Parents need informational, emotional, and social support during this time in order to adapt to the new role as the parent of a child with a disability. Some parents may feel vulnerable and will not share diagnostic information with the preschool, fearing the child may be asked to leave the school, or may not have the same preschool experience as other children. This is a true loss of dreams for parents. Another reason parents do not disclose a diagnosis is because of the concern they feel about the effects this stigma could have on their child. They often act as if nothing has changed or deny seeing any changes in their child's behavior. Chapter 22, "Understanding Families—The Impact of Disability" will help you understand the implications of this journey on parents.

As parents learn to understand the impact of disability on their child and on the family, caring support from their religious preschool can be helpful.

Some children will receive services through early childhood special education services and will leave your preschool. Some children will be able to attend preschool part time. Others will continue to attend with the same frequency as before the diagnosis.

A strong parent-professional partnership can resolve many

challenging situations. Parents value trusted allies. Good preschool collaboration sets the standard parents will expect throughout the child's school years. As long as you work together to support parents' hopes and dreams for the child, you will have a successful partnership with them. Use the *Parent Conference Preparation form* in this chapter and in the **Companion Workbook** to help parents identify and articulate what is important to them.

Do not make assumptions about a child's diagnosis, even in the spirit of showing support. One preschool brought in a developmental expert to observe a child who was having difficulty in their preschool class. The parents, notified by the preschool director *after* the observation, were upset. Although well intentioned, the preschool overlooked their responsibility to discuss the concerns they had with the parents and get permission in advance. The parents took the child out of the preschool and left the congregation.

Think collaboratively when working with parents. Parents and school professionals each bring their own perspectives to the collaboration, sharing important information about the child's home and school life, parent goals, and a wealth of professional experience.

Do not feel that you have to "fix" a situation on your own. As a team, parents and preschool professionals can work together to meet the needs and interests of each child. *No one does this alone.*

Work with parents to determine how to establish and maintain communication. Some schools stay in touch with parents through a proprietary website, giving updates on transitions, lunch, snacks, naps, and toileting. Email is another effective way. Whatever form of communication you decide to use, make sure there's written documentation. This will help evaluate the effectiveness of planned interventions.

Parent Conference Preparation Form

We will be collaborating to plan your child's program. Use both sides of this form. Please use this form to share your concerns, suggestions, and ideas, and to help us identify your child's strengths. Parents and staff will put their ideas together during the next conference.

Your Child's Name:
Date of Conference:

1. Overall, how do you think your child is doing at this time (around the house, in everyday places, etc.)?

2. Are there additional ways we can help meet your child's or family's needs, such as reading material, emotional support, contacts with other parents, equipment, information about community resources?

3. What other concerns or suggestions do you have?

4. Is there anything else you would like us to know?

Thank you for taking the time to fill out this form. The information you share will help us develop priorities and goals for your child's program at the upcoming conference. We value your input as members of the team.

Courtesy of St. Louis Park, MN Early Childhood Special Education Department and Bonnie Bogen

	What is going well?	What changes would you like to see?	Where should we work on these changes?		
			Home	School	Other
Coordination/ Getting around					
Communication					
Toy play (what he/she does) Please mention favorites					
Learning, thinking, understanding					
Getting along with others					
Feeding, dressing, hygiene					

Be patient. Parents have a difficult journey to navigate. The stronger the partnership with you, the more support they will feel.

Picture Schedules for Preschool Classrooms

A picture schedule is simply a series of graphic or photographic representations that show students how their day will unfold.

A calendar or daily schedule presented in pictures can help *all* preschoolers manage information about their day at preschool and at home. You can create a visual schedule for the entire preschool day, and review it with students during Circle Time at the beginning of the day, and at various points throughout the day. If a deviation from the regular schedule is noted on the picture schedule, you can address it with students while showing the picture.

Picture schedules benefit all children. Teachers can refer to the picture schedule time and again, while spoken communication may be forgotten. Children can take as much time as they need to process visual information. It can help preschoolers organize themselves and helps them transition from one activity to another.

Here are five tips for successful visual schedules.
1. Use real pictures that clearly reflect the activity.
2. Use pictures of real children without distracting props or backgrounds.
3. Display pictures from top to bottom (the way children naturally move, not left to right).
4. Include a "done pocket" for completed tasks.
5. Make sure the pictures/schedule only reflects the current task—and the ones left to complete.

Circle Time Scenarios

This Circle Time activity provides a sense of community and belonging for all children. Creating a scenario about each child's strengths, interests, and contributions to the class is a way for all children to feel they belong. Here is an example of a Circle Time Scenario.

> Eli goes to preschool four days a week with his younger brother Isaac. Eli is in the Pre-K class this year, which means that next year he is going to be old enough to go to kindergarten.
>
> Miss Allie is Eli's teacher, and she is nice. Eli likes Circle Time, and he likes to sit calmly in the circle and look at the teacher when she talks. He likes to listen to what Miss Allie says. If Eli has something to say, he tries to wait until the teacher calls on him. He raises his hand because he wouldn't like it if it were his turn to talk and someone else just talked because they felt like it. In Miss Allie's class, all of her students wait for their turn to be called on. If Eli has something important to say, and forgets to raise his hand, which we all do sometimes, Miss Allie gently tugs on her ear. That is the signal she and Eli worked out to remind him to raise his hand. Would you like a signal from your teacher to help remind you about something?
>
> Eli's favorite part of Circle Time is choosing jobs for the day. He likes being the line leader, and talking about the weather. The students take turns with the jobs because it wouldn't be fair if one person got to be the line leader all the time. Eli also likes when it's his turn to pick a Circle Time song.
>
> In Circle Time, Miss Allie shows the class pictures of the activities for the rest of the day. Eli likes the pictures because he knows what will happen in preschool that day.

Do you like our picture schedule?

Creating a scenario for every child gives each one of them a chance to shine. Peers learn about each other, and no one feels left out. Sharing a child's challenge, like when Eli forgets to raise his hand when he wants to be called on, and having a reminder to help him, lets all children know that school is a safe and non-judgmental place. The scenarios are a great way to share strengths, too. Creating the scenario around an ordinary part of the school day creates a common bond among the children.

Notice there is no reference to disability or labeling in the scenario. Children simply regard each other as peers and friends, accept differences and find common likes and interests.

Food for Thought:
- How could you further partner with parents of preschool students who have a developmental delay or diagnosis?
- What are some other classroom tools you use, or could use, to build on children's interests and strengths?

Chapter 16

INCLUSIVE RELIGIOUS EDUCATION

*Teach each child according to his way. Even
when he is old he will not depart from it.*

— Proverbs 22:6

I use the term "religious school" in this chapter to mean any entity
under the auspices of a faith community devoted to educating
children and teens. This includes day schools, and congregational
and community religious schools, and other educational programs.

Not so long ago, children with disabilities were often invisible
in religious educational settings. Some schools offered special
classes for children with disabilities. But more often, children with
a diverse spectrum of diagnoses never made it into the ranks of
religious education students.

When the U.S. Congress in 1975 passed Public Law 94-142,
also known as the Education for All Handicapped Children Act,
children with disabilities were included in public school
classrooms. The law was reauthorized in 1997 as the Individuals
with Disabilities Act (IDEA). "Parent power was one of the
forces that drove us to include children with disabilities in Jewish
education," said Dr. Sara Rubinow Simon, a pioneer in religious
special education. Over time parents recognized the benefits of
inclusion and they began to advocate for their children to attend
religious school with their peers without disabilities.

Growing numbers of religious schools now welcome students
with disabilities, and seek to provide meaningful and inclusive
academic experiences. In addition to providing religious education,

schools also promote social learning. Many children with disabilities or mental health conditions may not feel comfortable interacting with peers or may not understand the underlying social curriculum. Peer relationships can be hindered when students see only the differences in their peers with disabilities or don't know how to engage with them. When coupled with an individual's difficulty to understand social context, immediate barriers to friendship often develop. However, religious education provides a significant opportunity to accept differences, find common ground, and foster social inclusion.

The significant changes have taken years of advocacy by parents to include children with disabilities in religious education. Education is a major point of entry into lifelong community engagement. Faith communities cannot squander opportunities to educate children with disabilities. Outdated beliefs shut children out before they even step one foot through the school door.

As you read this chapter, consider how students with disabilities and mental health conditions are welcomed and supported in religious education.

- Do you provide aides for those who need support in the classroom? Are these aides volunteers or are they paid? Is there a line item in the budget to pay them?
- Do you assign students with different abilities, needs, and interests to work together?
- Do you train teachers to manage diverse learning styles?
- Do your registration forms ask parents to share information about their student's strengths and challenges?

Why Schools Don't Include Students with Disabilities

There are a number of reasons why some religious schools do not include students with disabilities in their classrooms and programs. Providing special education services can be costly. Some schools ask parents to pay for services such as one-to-one aides. Some schools are concerned that if they educate even one child with a disability, they might be overwhelmed by a deluge of students with complex needs and accommodations. Conversely, some religious schools purposely exclude students with disabilities, worried that other parents might decide to pull their students out, implying that inclusion negatively impacts the quality of education. Some parents choose not to send their children with disabilities to a religious school. Exhausted by the demands of raising a child with a disability, in addition to other family and work responsibilities, they have valid concerns. Does the school have experience teaching children with disabilities? Are their teachers trained to teach children with disabilities? Will the child be included with peers without disabilities? Will peers bully or make fun of the child? Can the child keep up with classmates? Will parents be required to pay extra fees for classroom aides? Will the school understand the child's strengths as well as his needs for support? Will parents constantly need to stay on top of everything?

A number of excellent books and websites provide information about the technical aspects of teaching children with diverse learning styles and disabilities. This chapter highlights the essential components that contribute to creating and maintaining a learning environment for all children. Many of the ideas will ignite a spark to begin or expand your current level of inclusion.

Parent-School Partnerships

Parent-school partnerships are at the heart of inclusive religious education.

Collaboration between parents and school staff makes a difference in the quality of education when they come together as a child-focused team. Each party brings expertise and experience. Most important, parents and school staff share the goal of a positive and meaningful religious school education. Dr. Sara Rubinow Simon said, "Learn what the child does well and how he or she can shine. All students need to feel the sense of accomplishment and success."

Sometimes parents don't disclose that their child has a disability, fearing rejection or labeling by the school. Still, having a disability can impact how a child learns and interacts with peers. Parents' reluctance to share information with educators comes up every time I work with school professionals, camp, and youth directors. Schools want parents to know that providing this information gives them a chance to work with the child to meet their needs and capitalize on their strengths and interests. This is the single most important aspect to parent-school relationships.

Use the following form, which is also in the **Companion Workbook**, for *each* child in your school as part of the registration process to learn about the child's learning, interests, strengths, and challenges.

Tell Us About Your Child

We have a wonderful year ahead of us—one filled with opportunities for growth for students of all ages. We believe that religious education is a birthright and a partnership between parents, students, and educators. Our goal is to provide a positive, substantive, and enduring learning experience for every student.

Each child has learning preferences, strengths, and challenges. Please provide information that will help us create a positive experience for your child.

Name of Your Student _____

Parent 1 Name _____

Parent 1 Cell _____

Parent 1 E-mail _____

Parent 2 Name _____

Parent 2 Cell _____

Parent 2 E-mail _____

What is the best way to communicate with you?

_____

_____

_____

What are your child's strengths as a learner?

_____

_____

_____

Please share any challenges your child faces in a learning environment.

_____

_____

_____

What are you most excited about for your child as they begin this religious school year?

_____

_____

_____

What concerns do you have?

_____

_____

_____

Would you like to schedule a meeting with us to discuss your concerns? _____

_____

_____

What is the best day and time to meet?

_____

Has your child been diagnosed with a disability? _____
If yes, please describe:

_____

_____

_____

Does your child have an IEP, 504 plan, or other type of accommodation at school? ☐Yes ☐No

_____

What else do you want us to know?

_____

_____

_____

Teacher Training to Support Diverse Learners

Many religious education teachers may not have formal training in education, or may not be familiar or comfortable teaching a diverse group of learners.

Provide mandatory training for your entire staff. Inclusion is the responsibility of everyone who interacts with students and families in the school. Training can ease some of their concerns and build confidence.

What Does Inclusion Mean in Your School?

Start training by providing concrete information about inclusion. It helps your educators acquire a basic and common understanding of inclusion, and what it means in your school and community. Share the school's vision for inclusion. Discuss the following and leave time for additional questions.

- What role do the teachers play?
- How will inclusion affect individual classrooms and teaching styles?
- How will inclusion change how you've done things in the past?
- Where do teachers find resources and support?

Give the teaching staff time to reflect on this new concept and encourage their questions.

Some schools include a session on teaching students with diverse needs as part of orientation in the fall.

- Discuss why inclusion is part of the school culture.
- Provide strategies on how to work with parents.
- Include tools to adapt or modify curriculum to meet students' varying readiness levels, learning preferences, and

interests.

- Emphasize that teachers do not need to have all the answers, or know precisely what to do in every situation. Identify people in the school or congregation who can help them.

Many schools devote time at weekly or monthly staff meetings to address an emerging concern, or cover a particular topic in depth. Ask the teaching staff to suggest topics that reflect activity in their classrooms. Sometimes it's helpful to hold a discussion and brainstorm strategies to overcome some of the concerns.

Think about other ways to support teachers in gaining competency and skills.

Teacher-to-Teacher Mentors

Teachers who have more experience can mentor a colleague who is starting out or doesn't have as much classroom or teaching experience. A mentor can be a sounding board, a voice of experience, and can encourage a teacher to experiment with different strategies. They can brainstorm solutions and provide support as ideas are implemented.

Teen Teaching Assistants

Many teens look forward to being a teaching assistant in religious education. Perhaps they remember a particular favorite teaching assistant from their younger days, are interested in sharing their knowledge, or are simply looking for a way to stay connected to their community.

Teen teaching assistants work closely with classroom teachers or school specialists to help with classroom management, music and art sessions, and work with students in small groups or one-to-one settings. Teen teaching assistants can be trained to work with students who have diverse learning needs, mental health conditions, or who need behavior support and guidance. Teen teaching assistants encourage younger students and can be positive role models.

One religious school requires all its teens to become teaching assistants. Some schools have teens go through an application process or let them choose to participate in the program on their own.

There are various ways to train teen teaching assistants. Schools can offer an elective course to teach teens the basics of being a teaching assistant. Some religious schools collaborate to train teens to work with students with disabilities in a year-long program. They meet for a full week of intensive training before the school year starts, and then meet once a month to cover specific topics.

Build a School Culture of Respect

The highlight of the year for fifth grade religious school students is the class play. Every student in the class gets to participate. During practice one day, several students stuck a sign on the back of a classmate with an intellectual disability. The sign said "KICK ME!" The students who stuck the sign on their classmate sniggered as he began to walk toward his place on the stage. Making fun of a vulnerable classmate who was unaware that he was the butt of their degrading joke was a form of bullying.

All his classmates saw the sign. Only one student did something about it. He gently removed the sign without his peer ever knowing it was there. He did this in full view of the other students and the teacher. After play practice, he told the principal what happened. The following school session, the class met with the principal for a serious conversation about how their actions constituted bullying.

The fifth grader who removed the sign stood up to the bullies, and showed the teacher and his classmates the values he'd been taught in school—to treat every person with dignity and respect. Religious schools, which naturally emphasize how to treat others, must teach students how to prevent bullying when they see it happening.

Inclusion goes beyond adapting teaching materials. In order to achieve an inclusive culture, we have to address things which make us feel uncomfortable. In doing so, we teach tolerance and acceptance, modeling how to stand up for ourselves and others. Schools must not permit behavior that hurts another person.

Do not let these times go by without making them teachable moments to develop an inclusive culture in your school.

Becoming an inclusive school happens one step at a time. Michelle Steinhart, a congregational inclusion director, told me that more than twenty years ago she was hired by the congregation to teach students with disabilities. At a time when religious schools were telling parents "No" when they asked if their child could attend, Michelle's school was saying "Yes." The congregation was passionate and committed to educating all children in its religious school. This one step paved the way over the years to create a genuinely inclusive school where each child is taught according to their abilities, and for the faith community at large to build an inclusive environment.

Food for Thought:
- Inclusion is not "one-size fits all." What do you believe the obstacles are to teaching a diverse body of students?
- How can you weave inclusion into the culture of your religious school?

Chapter 17

INCLUSION IN RELIGIOUS LIFE-CYCLE EVENTS

I will bless you, God, at all times, praise of the Highest will constantly be in my mouth. With you, my soul shines forth glory.
When the humble hear, they will rejoice.

— Psalm 34:1

Life-cycle celebrations mark an affirmation of faith, a parent's or individual's commitment to follow the practices of the religion and engage in the life of the community. These events are often recognized in individual or group ceremonies.

Many life-cycle events occur when a child reaches an age where he can affirm his faith. Congregations often have requirements and expectations for a child to prepare for a life-cycle event. Children with disabilities have often been left out of preparation and study for life-cycle events such as baptism, confirmation, and *Bar* or *Bat Mitzvah*. Exclusion was based on the assumption that children with disabilities could not learn, reason, understand, or believe, and therefore, could not affirm their faith in the traditional ways of the congregation.

Many parents of children with disabilities, feeling over-whelmed by daily responsibilities, medical appointments, school meetings, work, and caring for other children, did not have the energy to tackle one more thing. Often congregational requirements were rigid and did not allow flexibility for individual learning styles and abilities.

Some parents may assume because their child has a disability, she may not participate in life-cycle events. One parent was surprised when her rabbi called to discuss choosing a date for her son's *Bar Mitzvah* ceremony. She didn't think he could because of his disability. The rabbi reassured her that they would find a way to make this meaningful for her son, her family, and the congregation. The date was set and thus began a collaboration that ended with a meaningful and joyful ceremony marking this young man's becoming an adult in the eyes of his Jewish community.

When a congregation says "No" it is sending the message to parents that there is no place for their child. When parents hear that one member of their family is not welcome, they may feel the entire family is not welcome and search for a community where they are all accepted. Or, sadly they may leave their faith entirely.

This chapter describes adapting life-cycle events to leverage a person's strengths and meet their needs. You can modify the information to express your own faith tradition to teach and prepare children, as well as adults, for life-cycle celebrations. The goal is to ensure that every individual has the opportunity to participate in their faith tradition. It also will help you understand what it means to individuals and families to celebrate life-cycle events with their community.

Successful Life-Cycle Celebrations

Life-cycle ceremonies of children who have disabilities are always very moving and emotional for the child's parents, family members, friends, and their faith community. When a child is diagnosed with a disability, this particular dream may seem elusive as parents begin to learn about the diagnosis and how it might impact their child.

Congregations must be committed to including all children in life-cycle education and celebrations. The keys to success are understanding an individual's style of learning, adapting the curriculum, and maintaining communication between parents, clergy, teachers, tutors, and the individual. The preparation process can be enormously enriching for everyone involved.

To the greatest extent possible, children with disabilities should be included with their peers without disabilities for confirmation, and other group celebrations.

When assigning responsibilities to students, don't assume that a child with a disability will be unable to do what their peers without disabilities can do. Meet with the parents and the child to discuss the child's strengths, concerns about how to adapt learning materials, and demonstrating what they have prepared for at the service. No one can predict how well the child will do until they're given the opportunity.

Each child will be different. Match them with a tutor or teacher who is flexible and supportive, works well with diverse learning styles, and communicates well with parents, the congregation, and school staff.

Many children are nervous or intimidated when they begin studying for such an important occasion. With thoughtful guidance, children with disabilities will be able to understand and make meaning of important religious milestones in their lives.

This can be a time of incredible growth and development for children with disabilities.

Tutoring and Teaching Tips

The clergy and tutor, or group teacher, should meet with parents and the child, as appropriate, to discuss strengths, abilities, interests, and challenges. It helps when parents share their child's school Individual Education Program (IEP) as it can provide strategies to teach the child. Also use the "Tell Us About Your Child" format on page 209 and in the **Companion Workbook.**

Teach students to their abilities and strengths as learners

- For auditory learners, record the materials so students can use them on their phone.
- Enlarge reading materials for students with visual disabilities.
- Discuss the text a student is preparing to read or chant so they understand it and how it applies to life today.
- Invite parents to lessons from time to time, with the student's permission, so they can observe their child's progress.
- Use visual schedules to teach the order of the service.
- Work closely with your child's team, to update them about progress and how accommodations are working. Discuss any challenges you encounter as a team.
- Provide an adult or a peer who the student is comfortable with to assist them during the ceremony.
- Recognize a student's achievements at each class. Try stickers or stars. For some children, a good motivator is something they love, like baseball cards. Talk with the parents about providing a supply.
- Adapt the Weekly Homework Form in the **Companion Workbook** to record assignments. Break homework down into manageable steps, how much time to spend on each, and record them in columns marked Assignment A, B, and C. I use this form with my own *Bar* and *Bat Mitzvah* students who need structure. There's even a column for

parents to initial every day their child practices.

- Before rehearsals, give the student several opportunities to hold ritual items used in the service, stand on the pulpit, and practice their parts in the service.
- Prepare the student for their ceremony by practicing the entire service several times before the actual rehearsal.

Another Life-Cycle Celebration

Celebrating with Bride and Groom

People with disabilities fall in love. The intimacy of marriage, building a life together, and becoming a family are a part of many peoples' definition of a quality life. Celebrating in the couple's faith community is another life-cycle event. It starts long before the bride and groom exchange wedding vows and rings.

The marriage preparation and support you typically offer should be provided for couples where one or both have a disability. It's important to get to know the couple and learn about their hopes and dreams for their future together. Offering guidance, including them in marriage preparation classes, and discussing their religious beliefs builds a holy relationship that will endure throughout their lifetime together.

Several years ago I went to the funeral of a young woman who lived with a disability. She had married the love of her life a year earlier. Her husband also had a disability. The eulogy by her pastor was a portrait of a determined and accomplished woman whose joy in life increased when she fell in love and was married. Still a bride when she died, she was buried in her wedding dress.

In Chapter 23, "Supporting People in Difficult Times," I address the final life-cycle event, death and mourning.

Food for Thought:
- List the life-cycle events of your faith tradition. How are people with disabilities and mental health conditions supported in their preparations and in the ceremonies?
- Many people say that attending a life-cycle event of a person with a disability or mental health condition is so moving, for example, "There wasn't a dry eye in the place!" Why do you think that is the case?

Chapter 18

YOUTH GROUP BELONGING AND INCLUSION

At the core of being an adolescent is an inherent insecurity and constant wondering how and where one truly belongs. Teens with disabilities are no different in this from their non-disabled peers.

– Lisa Friedman,
Youth and Community Inclusion Expert

Pre-teens and teens with disabilities or mental health conditions want to belong. They want to participate in the social activities of faith community life like their peers. Abundant opportunities exist in youth groups. Making friends, and participating with peers in sports, the arts, hobbies, as well as embracing other interests such as social justice causes, or acquiring leadership skills are just a few ways to belong.

Living with a disability or mental health condition should not be an obstacle to participation. Parents of teens lament about how difficult it is for their children to feel they belong. Obstacles range from expecting parents to pay for additional support staff at youth and recreational programs to youth leaders telling them outright that their child is "too disabled" to participate. We can, and must, eliminate the beliefs, attitudes, and practices from all recreational programs that exclude or minimize participation by adolescents with disabilities and mental health conditions.

Belonging to a youth group can have a positive effect on

physical, intellectual, social, and emotional well-being. Youth groups can also have a lasting impact on all participants.

A teen who lives with a disability or mental health condition needs opportunities to make choices based on their interests, like anyone else. Providing individual supports creates opportunities to feel a strong sense of belonging and contribution.

Youth Group Inclusion

Belonging to a group of peers is important for just about everyone. Building friendships, learning, taking part in social action, and developing leadership skills are all important benefits of youth group participation. Religious youth groups can also keep teens engaged in their faith community.

Youth inclusion expert Lisa Friedman urges congregations to create teen engagement opportunities that are meaningful and content-rich. Even when this is done well, the primary reason teens drop out is that they feel they don't have any friends in the program.

Train Youth Group Staff

Professional development for the staff is necessary. Appropriate training increases staff competence and skills which foster an inclusive culture and support teens with disabilities and mental health conditions. Training should raise awareness about the importance of belonging and what that means to all teens. To advance a culture of belonging and inclusion, also invite members of the youth committee to participate so they are on the same page as the staff.

Begin by scheduling a three-hour block of time devoted to training around the basics of inclusion. From *Longing to Belonging* has many practical resources for training and youth group inclusion. Invite the inclusion committee to partner with you.

- Review Chapter 3, "Even Moses Needed a Voice" for definitions of inclusion and disability.
- Review Chapter 4, "Obstacles and Opportunities," which highlights the most common obstacles to participation and inclusion.
- Share the youth group assessment conducted by the inclusion committee. Ask participants to share their perspectives on the opportunities they see.
- Read Chapter 5, "The Spirit of Belonging" before attending training, as this is the cornerstone for youth inclusion. Discuss what it means to each person to belong. Have them brainstorm what they can do to foster belonging.
- Hands-on experience is a great teacher. Using the "Spirit of Belonging Questions" on page 79 and 80 as prompts, pair participants, and give each pair fifteen minutes to have a conversation. Follow up with a discussion about how it felt to ask and answer the questions, and how having these types of conversations with youth participants can have a positive effect on inclusion and participation.

Follow-up to Training

Gabrielle Kaplan-Mayer, a specialist in youth group training, suggests identifying disability and inclusion experts in the congregation or community to mentor youth leaders. Ask the inclusion committee if there are people on the committee who could fulfill this role.

Youth leaders will benefit from training on how to work with parents. Work with the inclusion committee on how to address this sensitive topic. Read Chapter 22, "Understanding Families—The Impact of Disability," then invite a parent panel to share their experiences and discuss effective strategies.

Plan for Success

Planning is another key to successful youth group inclusion. Many youth events tend to be less structured and formal.

Overnight retreats generally contain a fair amount of downtime. Unstructured time can be challenging for some teens. Leaders can review retreat schedules looking for unstructured times as well as social expectations. With this information, youth leaders can best consider how to support them. Gabrielle Kaplan-Mayer suggests offering structured alternatives, pairing teens, and creating activities based on the interests of participants with a disability. They can also help lead the activity or share their knowledge and skills with the group.

Practical Strategies to Including Teens with Disabilities and Mental Health Conditions

- Include your inclusion and accommodations statements when you publicize all of your activities.
- Follow through when people request an accommodation.
- Meet with new teens before their first event so they are familiar with at least one person. Everyone wants the assurance they will be welcomed and included. Get to know the teen's interests and talents, and also learn what makes him feel nervous or uncertain. This is a good strategy to incorporate for all youth group members. You can also turn this into an activity, pairing peers to learn more about each other, and sharing non-confidential information with the group.

- Observe new teens during events. What do they seem to enjoy doing? What are they good at doing? You may have a budding assistant director for your next play— or a new prayer leader in your midst.
- Make sure all events are accessible.
- Write an article for your organization's newsletter describing ways your youth program is committed to including teens with disabilities and mental health conditions.
- If your youth group goes to cultural events, such as community plays, make sure you attend when there is a signed performance if you have a participant who uses American Sign Language (ASL).
- Offer an ASL-signed performance for your own youth group play, and advertise it.
- When arranging an outside event, such as bowling, find out if the bowling alley has a ball ramp so people with physical disabilities can bowl.
- Build a circle of friends for someone who's new to the group. Anyone coming to an event as a new participant may feel alone. Invite several teens to be part of the circle. They can welcome the new person, make introductions, initiate conversations with others in the group, and explain the lay of the land.
- Work with the inclusion committee to lead a service that focuses on inclusion.
- Partner with other youth organizations in your area to host a disability awareness conference.

- Brainstorm different ways to encourage teens with disabilities to participate and belong.

Listen to Teens with Disabilities and Mental Health Conditions

We can learn by listening to the teens themselves. Some adolescents with disabilities and mental health conditions are at risk for social isolation because they may not feel acceptance from peers. Their leisure activities tend to be passive and solitary. However, many teens are aware that having a disability is just one aspect of their lives and are eager to be actively involved in your youth group. Social and recreational activities provide opportunities to build peer connections that lead to friendship and acceptance.

Teens who live with a disability or a mental health condition want to be accepted and included.

Parents and service providers may assume to know what adolescents with disabilities want. Asking teens what *they* want empowers them to share their interests, strengths, and hopes. Assuming teens with disabilities are essentially different from peers without disabilities can have negative consequences. Assumptions lead to low expectations, isolation from peers and diminish feelings of belonging.

Friendship and Social Connection

Social inclusion is often the most difficult aspect of participation for many people with disabilities and mental health conditions. Think of different ways to draw teens in.

A good place to start is by asking teens what they enjoy doing.

How can you encourage them to share those talents, gifts, and strengths with the youth group?

These are just a few ideas you can use to break down individual barriers:

- Provide frequent and consistent opportunities for all youth group participants to get acquainted.
- Form small groups or pairs and create opportunities for teens to get to know each other.
- Use ice breakers.
- Wear name tags.
- Mix up the groups often.
- Give information in several formats.
- Promote equal status among youth group members by reminding them that everyone is part of making decisions and participating in activities. Focus on teamwork to reinforce the equal status.
- Use a cooperative structure where each person completes a part of the whole.
- Break down activities into smaller steps.
- Instill the Spirit of Belonging—everyone plays, everyone is valued.
- Build cooperation and interdependence.
- Keep verbal communication clear.

Food for Thought:

- How are teens with disabilities and mental health conditions involved in youth programs now? After reading this chapter, what can your organization do to promote the Spirit of Belonging?

- Identify opportunities to increase participation of teens with disabilities and mental health conditions in leadership roles in your youth organization.

Chapter 19

CAMP AND RECREATIONAL INCLUSION

Anyone who has ever had the privilege to attend summer camp will often say, "Camp is where I get to be my best self." Summer camp is also an opportunity for us to experience our communal "best self." This is especially true when there is a vibrant disability inclusion program.

— Lisa Handelman,
Camp and Community Disability Inclusion Specialist

Including children with disabilities and mental health conditions in summer camp builds a strong community in a more informal setting than during the school year. In school, children must cope with homework, testing, therapies, and other demands. Summer camp can be more relaxed. However, stressors such as adapting to new schedules and routines, living with other children at overnight camp, transitioning between activities, and learning how to interact with new peer groups and adults can be challenging. The keys to a successful summer involves building trusting relationships between parents and camp staff, providing appropriate supports, and getting to know each child.

Lisa Handelman is the inclusion coordinator at Capitol Camps, an overnight camp in the Washington, D.C. area. From the beginning, Capitol Camps has welcomed campers with disabilities in all aspects of camp. Supports are provided based on what children, with and without disabilities need, *not* on a medical diagnosis.

Lisa points out the intersection between inclusion, values, and creating our best selves. "When we provide a camper with extra support to help him negotiate peer interactions so, like his peers, he can write home and say, 'Sorry I do not have time to write. I am too busy playing with my friends' we demonstrate Proverb 26, *'Teach each child according to his way.'*"

Encourage Parents to Share Information

During the first week of an overnight camp session, six children were added to the list of those who required accommodations or support. The inclusion specialist reviewed the information forms their parents submitted. None of the forms indicated that their children had a disability or mental health condition. None of the parents mentioned that their child received special education services at school. Camp for each of these children got off to a rocky start as staff scurried to figure out how to provide the support each camper needed.

A common concern among camps is that some parents do not share information that can help camp staff support their child. Why don't parents of children with disabilities disclose this information on camp information forms?

Parents send their children to summer camp for a variety of reasons. Camp can expose children to different activities they do not experience at home. Camp provides opportunities to meet new friends and try new things—rope climbing, swimming, boating, music, and drama. Camp is simply a different experience than school, and some parents feel their child had enough "special" services during the school year.

Some parents do not share information about their child's disability or mental health condition because they may have difficulty adjusting to the diagnosis. They may be uncomfortable talking about it, and may not be aware that sharing information could enhance the child's camp experience. Parents sometimes don't disclose because they think their child will be labeled and ostracized.

How can professionals help parents feel comfortable sharing information that will help create a positive camp experience? What builds positive and lasting partnerships between parents and camp?

Here are a few ways to encourage parents to share information.

Welcome Statement

Incorporate an inclusion statement on camp or program brochures, and on information-request forms. This helps parents feel more comfortable knowing the staff is committed to a productive partnership with them.

Think about what your statement conveys. Keep it simple.

"Summer camp provides the opportunity for children of all abilities to participate together. Inclusion benefits everyone."

"Camp _____ provides an inclusive environment for our campers. We welcome campers of all abilities."

Add language to encourage parents to share information with you.

"Each child's success at camp starts with a strong parent-camp relationship. Please share information about your child that will help us support them in camp life."

Many national, secular, and religious camping organizations have forms you can use, or adapt, to request information in a positive way. Some organizations meet with parents and children ahead of camp to learn more about the child and build partnerships with parents. Getting information in person rather than on a form is a much more productive way to ease parents' anxiety about a new experience. Use video conferencing if you are unable to be in the same location.

"Tell me about your child."

Start the conversation getting to know your potential camper or participant. Ask parents what goals they have for summer camp. Ask them to tell you about the child's interests, strengths, and what they like to do their spare time. Get a picture of what motivates them.

Then you can discuss accommodations, transitions and unexpected changes in schedules, and what makes the child feel comfortable and safe. Determine how to communicate with each other, and how often.

You can use the following questions to start the conversation with parents. The questions are also located in the **Companion Workbook**.

Tell Me About Your Child

Child's Name _____

Parent/Caregiver 1 Name _____

Parent/Caregiver 1 Cell _____

Parent/Caregiver 1 E-mail _____

Parent/Caregiver 2 Name _____

Parent/Caregiver 2 Cell _____

Parent/Caregiver 2 E-mail _____

1. What is your preferred method of communication?
    Phone, email, text? _____

2. Has your child been to camp before this summer?
    ❏Yes ❏No

3. Has your child participated in similar activities?

4. What did your child like? What didn't your child like?

5. What did you think about the experience?

6. What are your hopes for your child at camp?

7. Do you have any specific goals for your child at camp?

8. What is your child looking forward to at camp?

9. What concerns does your child have about going to camp?

10. What makes your child feel successful?

11. What interests does your child have?

12. What does your child do in his/her spare time?

13. How does your child communicate his/her feelings?

14. How do you know if your child feels anxious, nervous, uncertain, fearful, happy, content, excited?

15. How do you help your child manage his/her feelings?

16. How does your child let you know what he/she needs?

17. How does your child let others know if he/she needs something—for example, a break from the activity, a quiet space, comfort?

18. What can help your child manage transitions from activity to activity, or changes in routines?

19. What works to motivate your child? What doesn't work?

20. What works to help your child interact with peers? Does he/she have a preference for being in small or large groups, or one-to-one conversations?

21. Does your child receive any services during the school year, such as special education or additional support? Is there an Individualized Education Program (IEP) or 504 plan?

22. Would you be willing to share this with me? ☐Yes ☐No

23. Is there anything else you'd like to share with me at this time?

Inclusion Coordinator

More camps are hiring a designated staff member to coordinate and manage different aspects of inclusion and support for campers with disabilities and mental health conditions. The inclusion coordinator may work directly with campers, communicate with parents, problem-solve with front line staff, meet with parents and campers before camp starts, and lead staff training on inclusion.

The following list of responsibilities will help your camp consider the role of an inclusion coordinator, and the skills and experience required. Decide if this will be a seasonal or full time position.

The inclusion coordinator may be responsible to:

- Develop and facilitate pre-camp inclusion training for all staff.
- Provide more intensive training for staff who support campers with disabilities.
- Create forms and questionnaires to obtain information.
- Coordination information from parents, teachers, and outside agencies (e.g., medical professionals and government support agencies).
- Maintain parent contact before, during, and after the camp session.
- Interview/hire staff members to support campers with disabilities.
- Design modifications to programs and activities to accommodate children with disabilities.
- Provide ongoing training and support to specialists, unit heads, faculty, health center, and kitchen staff.
- Serve on the camp crisis management team.
- Document all aspects of the inclusion program.

- Maintain ongoing coordination of information gathered, anecdotal notes, scheduling, programing, outside contacts, and follow-up.
- Develop and implement behavior supports.
- Provide short and long-term support of staff members who have disabilities.
- Design individual work placements for staff with disabilities and ongoing task analysis.
- Work collaboratively with the camp director on camp inclusion, health and safety, camper issues, and staff morale.
- Model and advocate acceptance and understanding for campers and staff with disabilities and mental health conditions.

Manage Obstacles to Inclusion

Ask your staff to read Chapter 4 "Obstacles and Opportunities" to become familiar with the different types of obstacles. At a staff training or meeting, discuss the obstacles at camp and how they can be avoided or overcome.

Discuss the following questions with your staff. Add your own questions to address concerns and increase awareness.

- How might less accessible facilities hinder participation by someone with a physical disability? Walk through your facility with someone who has a mobility disability. See if there are programming areas that are not accessible. Move programs to accessible spaces. If you are considering making changes to the building or grounds, contact your state disability resources office to receive a copy of the state's accessibility survey. Ask if they offer training to organizations interested in renovating their facility.

- What is the focus of your programs? Is it winning? Having fun? Building self-acceptance and confidence? Making friends? If you have programs specifically for people with disabilities, start thinking inclusively. How do you make those programs more inclusive? What happens in those programs that others in your community would enjoy?

Base programs on what people want, not what they can do.

Food for Thought:
- What obstacles might prevent moving toward a more inclusive model? What is your first step to overcome them?
- What are some ways that you can grow more confident and comfortable supporting campers/participants/staff with disabilities and mental health conditions?

Chapter 20

LIFELONG LEARNING AND LIVING IN THE COMMUNITY

We have technology, know how, and ability so those of us with differences can lead productive and fulfilling lives. This requires reframing—getting away from the deficit/disorder/disability model and transitioning to the ability-based model, which asks, "What can the person do?" Let's make this the rule, and not the exception.

-Dr. Stephen Shore, EdD.,
Internationally known educator, consultant, and presenter on issues related to the autism spectrum

Adults with disabilities and mental health conditions want the same opportunities to live satisfying lives in the community as anyone else. They get to make their own life decisions. Some people may ask for input from family members, caregivers, and service providers, but there is a trap in assuming all people with disabilities and mental health conditions want or need it.

Relationships and promoting community engagement are two of the most critical factors in leading a fulfilling life for people living with a disability or mental health condition. Inclusion is not something that happens because we say it should. Inclusion is intentional. The Spirit of Belonging provides the mindset and the tools to build relationships. In a supportive relationship, individuals with a disability or mental health condition express what they want while others provide support.

Jay Ruderman is the president of the Ruderman Family Foundation. In a personal communication, Jay explained why his foundation has become a leader in the disability inclusion movement. "As we learned more about disability and inclusion, we came to view disability inclusion as a matter of civil rights. Seventy percent of people with disabilities are unemployed, and people with disabilities are, disproportionately, likely to live in poverty; and lack access to quality health care and education. From this civil-rights perspective, disability inclusion is not charity—it is what enables people with disabilities to access their basic civil and human rights. Disability inclusion benefits everyone, as it creates a society in which more people are working, voting, and contributing. This is the philosophy that guides our work. We know that by creating more inclusive institutions, we are strengthening our communities, and enabling all of us to reach our full potential."

This chapter examines several life domains in which faith-based organizations can support an individual's self-defined quality of life—faith community participation, employment opportunities, and life in the community.

Supports Impact Inclusion and Community Participation

First, let's examine how supporting someone can have a positive impact in the lives of people with disabilities or mental health conditions. The Council on Quality and Leadership (CQL) consults with communities, systems, and organizations to help support people with disabilities, people with mental health conditions, and older adults. In a study, CQL interviewed over 1300 people to determine how organizational support encourages and facilitates inclusion.[1]

When organizations support people to develop, maintain, and enhance friendships, people with disabilities are eighteen times more likely to have friends. That is significant. Friendships and relationships are the basis for natural support, and encourage an individual's fulfillment of self-determined outcomes based on what matters most to them.

CQL concluded, "People achieve their personal goals to become included in the community when the people who support them

- Get to know them,
- Take action to support them, and
- Work together to make things happen."

What are you waiting for? Let's get started!

Inclusive Participation in Faith Community Life

A faith community provides spiritual, social, religious, and educational opportunities for people of all ages with disabilities and mental health conditions. People who have participated in educational and religious experiences as children and teens cannot be forgotten. Many adults languish without the connections and relationships that marked childhood and adolescence. Adults can flourish, however, when they participate in faith community life.

Lifelong learning and living goes beyond adult education programs, worship services, and social events. People with disabilities have talents, skills, and interests to share as volunteers, committee members, prayer leaders, teachers, and many other roles. People feel a sense of belonging when they are involved in activities that are personally important and meaningful.

Early in my career, a community member who used a wheelchair asked me to start a support group for people with physical disabilities. I agreed. After all, this is what he told me he wanted.

I quickly thought of two other people who lived with physical disabilities. I invited them to come to a meeting. They all arrived at the appointed time, and there I was sitting at the head of the table telling them what my agenda was for their group.

One of the attendees was offended by the very idea of a group *for* people based on a disability label and said what she really wanted was to be part of a young adult group in her congregation. The two other people tapped into how they wanted to participate in their faith communities. The meeting quickly transformed from a group for people with physical disabilities to a conversation about determining the direction of their lives based on interests, hopes, strengths, and goals.

A valuable lesson—we don't do things *for* adults with disabilities and mental health conditions.
We do things *with* them.

The Spirit of Belonging is the driving force. The opportunities in the congregation are not any different for people with disabilities and mental health conditions than they are for anyone else. If someone wants to go to Bible study or take a class, just ask them if there is anything they need to participate.

Liz Weintraub is a senior advocacy specialist at the Association of University Centers on Disabilities (AUCD) and hosts the podcast, "Tuesdays With Liz: Disability Policy For All."

Liz and her husband Phil, who both live with disabilities, are very active in their religious community. She loves her congregation, she said, not only for the religious aspects, but how the community includes them. Liz and Phil participate in all parts of community life including congregational trips. While on a congregational trip to Italy, Liz received word that her father died. Being with her congregation at such a moment brought her comfort. She said, "I can't tell you how special that was, feeling included. From the moment I found out the news, people were ready to give me a hug."

Liz summed up what belonging means to her. "I feel like I belong when I am *part* of activities and trips that *everyone* participates in."

Volunteer Opportunities

Volunteers are a vital part of most faith communities. People with disabilities can volunteer in a lot of ways—as prayer and worship leaders, board and committee members, teachers, ushers, and event planners. Don't automatically assign people tasks *you think they can do*, such as being a greeter or joining the inclusion committee. Work with people to learn what interests them.

Dr. Stephen Shore said, "Focus on the strengths of the individual and use the motivating power behind the special interests we all have. Ask someone how they spend most of their time. We tend to spend most of our time doing things we like to do—we're good at them. Everyone who's successful has found a way to match their special interest with something that society values."

Learning Opportunities

Adult education opens up many avenues to participate and

belong. People with disabilities can participate in any of the adult learning programs you offer, including Bible study, congregational or community trips, life-cycle preparation event opportunities, social justice groups, and more. When you publicize adult education opportunities, remember to include an accommodation statement. See Appendix B, "Accessibility Statements and Accommodations Requests" for examples.

Tips for Learning Opportunities

- Add disability and mental health subjects to your adult education curriculum. Discuss how people with disabilities are regarded in the Bible and in your faith tradition.
- Some adults with disabilities may not have participated in age-appropriate life-cycle celebrations while growing up. Include them in adult life-cycle preparation classes. If you don't offer classes, work with people individually to prepare for a ceremony.
- As you get to know people, ask them what they would like to learn. For example, someone who is not familiar with the liturgy might be interested in a class on the topic. It's possible other people would also like to attend the class.
- Many faith communities offer trips to holy sites and mission work. When planning trips, take accessibility into account. There are tour providers who know accessible routes, lodging, and transportation, and specialize in creating accessible tours.

Faith Communities and Pathways to Employment

Faith communities can provide points of entry and establish

connections and networks that enhance quality of life. Competitive employment is an important consideration for many people who live with a disability or mental health condition.

Community members can connect people to jobs, training, and networks leading to employment. They can also support people who want to develop their entrepreneurial dreams and talents to start businesses. Look around your faith community—who is a business owner, hiring or human resources manager, or could provide information for people looking for jobs or business opportunities in particular fields?

The U.S. Department of Labor Office of Disability Employment Policy (ODEP) April 2018 Disability Employment report highlights the significant gap between people with and without disabilities.[2] Labor force participation by people with disabilities was 20.9 percent, compared to 68.3 percent for people without disabilities. The unemployment rate was 10.5 percent for people with disabilities compared to 4.6 percent for people without disabilities.

Public policy at the federal level has shifted from sheltered workshops, which hire only people with disabilities at sub-minimum wages, to employment in the most integrated setting appropriate at, or above, minimum wage. In this setting, people with and without, disabilities can interact and work together.

The Collaborative on Faith and Disabilities at Vanderbilt University and the Kessler Foundation developed *Putting Faith to Work* (PFTW). Piloted in twenty-seven congregations around the United States, PFTW is built on developing the capacity of faith communities to support people with disabilities to find and maintain employment. This strength-based approach focuses on individual gifts, skills, and passions. The Collaborative on Faith and

246 - Shelly Christensen

Disabilities has developed a step-by-step manual for faith communities which is available on their website.[3]

Faith communities can hire people with disabilities. Hiring a person with a disability is *not* an act of kindness or charity. Hiring decisions are based on a person's qualifications for the position. The ADA gives specific guidelines for hiring candidates with disabilities, including what questions can be asked during their interview. The complete guide to the interview and hiring process of Title I of the ADA is located on the Jobs Accommodation Network website.[4]

A Little Background on Community-Based Living

The landmark passage of the Americans with Disabilities Act (ADA) in 1990 codified the rights of all Americans with disabilities to lead lives of their own choosing, without being subjected to discrimination. Under the ADA, people with disabilities have the right to equal treatment by being given access to support which allows them to fully participate in community life.

In the United States, federal regulations for funding long-term care of people with disabilities also stipulates the rights of people to live in the community as they choose. Deborah Fisher, Psy.D., a former executive in residential and support services who now consults with service provider agencies, said, "These requirements go so far as to say that housing providers, along with support services, have to protect people's rights to live where, how, and with whom they want, through an annual lease. People with disabilities have demanded this. The U.S. Congress, the Supreme Court, and funding and regulatory agencies have responded by ensuring access to fully engaged lives through the support of people, services, and communities. Our challenge as family members, taxpayers, neighbors, congregants, and friends is to secure the resources needed to protect and promote these recent gains."

In 1999, the United States Supreme Court ruling in *Olmstead v. L.C.* recognized unjustified institutional isolation of persons with disabilities as a form of discrimination.[5] It reflects two judgments. The first judgment is that "institutional placement of persons who can handle and benefit from community settings perpetuates unwarranted assumptions that persons so isolated are incapable or unworthy of participating in community life." The second judgment is that "confinement in an institution severely diminishes the everyday life activities of individuals, including family relations, social contacts, work options, economic independence, educational advancement, and cultural enrichment."

Dr. Fisher said, "We have moved people from institutions and achieved huge human rights successes for all people. People with disabilities are asking that they be treated with the same respect and dignity as people without disabilities are treated."

The Centers for Medicare and Medicaid Services (CMS) Home and Community Based Services (HCBS) Settings Rule provides that all settings where people receive HCBS services must:

- Be chosen by the person from options that include non-disability specific settings and a private unit.
- Be integrated into, and support access to, the greater community.
- Provide opportunities to seek employment in integrated settings, engage in community life, and control personal resources.
- Give the same degree of access to services in the community as those not receiving HCBS.[6]

Dr. Fisher said, "This means supporting an individual's desires and dreams to live as valued members of their communities exercising their rights to choose where, with whom, and how they want to live. They want to select the staff who support them based on compatibility."

Most adults with intellectual and developmental disabilities still live in their family homes. Parents' concerns over the safety of living in the community, the cost of housing, and finding compatible support staff are some of the reasons adults with disabilities don't move out. But as parents age, they must face the reality of what will happen to their adult child when they can no longer care for them.

"Nothing about us without us!" expresses the belief that people with disabilities and mental health conditions must be at the table from the beginning for any planning and decision-making. They are the experts on their own lives.

Faith Communities and Pathways into Community Life

Sheryl Grossman, a Jewish Orthodox disabled woman and board chair of *Yad HaChazakah*, the Jewish Disability Empowerment Center, is very active in her faith community, and advises faith-based organizations on adult inclusion and belonging. Sheryl discussed the responsibility faith communities have to support an individual with a disability or mental health condition. She said, "You have to meet people where they are at. Faith communities have the obligation to remove the stumbling block to allow those in our midst to succeed within our community."

Sheryl asked, "Are you handing someone fish or are you teaching them to fish?" In other words, the role of faith communities is to help people to live how, where, and with whom they want.

Friendship is the all-important foundation. Sheryl said, "It's on the community to stop discriminating and to put hesitancy aside to be with a person with a disability on a friendship level. Let's start talking and get to know each other. When you become someone's new friend you start out learning about each other, sharing personal stories, and trusting each other. Stop being afraid of the other. Actually listen and become a part of each other's lives."

Dr. Shana Erenberg has spent her entire professional life supporting people with disabilities. Her private practice provides diagnostic evaluation, remediation, and advocacy for children and adults with disabilities. When there is a need for action, Dr. Erenberg is there.

Dr. Erenberg founded *Libenu* (Our Hearts) to support children and adults with disabilities and their families living in Chicago. Dr. Erenberg describes *Libenu* as a "Yes, and…" organization. Individuals define their hopes and dreams, and determine what is important to them. "*Libenu* supports them by helping to think outside of the box and then providing person-centered services to help them succeed," said Dr. Erenberg, who believes there's always more than one way to reach a goal.

Supporting someone means making a commitment to truly understand what individuals with disabilities want in life, and finding innovative means to enable them to fulfill their dreams and actualize their potential.

Dr. Erenberg suggests the following steps to engage adults in your faith community:

- First, and foremost, ask the individual what he or she wants to learn or do in terms of his or her practice. Be mindful of how you ask — not everyone can process or respond in the same way.

- Provide educational opportunities for the individual to acquire the requisite skills, both practical and social, to be successful in his or her practice.
- Structure, sequence, and teach the steps of each task.
- Continuously monitor and evaluate how the person is progressing, using feedback to inform and improve your instruction.

Liane Kupferberg Carter, author of *Ketchup is My Favorite Vegetable: A Family Grows Up with Autism,* described the importance of the faith community for her adult son, Mickey. "Mickey is twenty-five now. He will be an autistic adult much longer than he was an autistic child, and he's going to need a lot of things like safe housing, social services, and employment opportunities. But most of all? He needs a community that truly welcomes him, and we're still not there yet. We need to keep sharing our voices, our passion, our commitment, until Mickey and everybody else who's differently-abled is welcome at the table."[7]

When a faith community comes alongside a person with a disability or mental health condition it says, "You belong to this community." There is work to do, and the day is short. We cannot be satisfied with waiting till the right time, because that time is now.

Food for Thought?
- Select one of the areas discussed in this chapter. How can your faith community be more supportive and involved in this area?
- How can you make sure that people with disabilities and mental health conditions have the opportunity to make their own decisions?

Chapter 21

SUPPORTING PEOPLE WITH MENTAL HEALTH CONDITIONS

When you go through deep waters I will be with you.
— Isaiah 48:2

In my job as program manager of the Jewish Community Inclusion Program for People with Disabilities, I was charged with the mission to include people with intellectual, developmental, and physical disabilities. I did a lot of public speaking over the years. Occasionally an audience member would approach me, usually hanging back until everyone else had spoken to me, to ask if the program included people living with a mental health condition.

I felt uncomfortable answering the question. I could see hope in the people's eyes, and I did not want to disappoint them and say "No." After all, inclusion means everyone. Doesn't it?

I danced around the question, never really giving a definitive answer. I did not know what to say. I referred people to a mental health project in my agency or toward therapeutic resources, and put the whole thing out of my mind.

Until a mental health diagnosis affected me personally. I was diagnosed with depression well into my adulthood. It was then I realized that I had lived with depression and anxiety since I was a teen. At first, it was difficult to talk about it outside of my immediate family and closest friends. Slowly, I began to share my experiences, and found strength in knowing I was not alone.

When we view inclusion through the lens of "belonging," we can deconstruct the stigma associated with mental health conditions and people's lived experiences. According to Dr. Mark Salzer, Director of the Temple University Collaborative on Community Inclusion, there is some debate about the use of the term "stigma" as it refers to a "mark of shame." Dr. Salzer said, "Some suggest simply using (the words) prejudice and discrimination, which are also much more direct. Nonetheless, 'stigma' remains a commonly used word."

When we educate ourselves about the prevalence of people diagnosed with mental health conditions, it's clear that clergy, lay leaders, and congregants can play an important role in supporting people to increase their sense of belonging and remove the stigma.

The Facts About Mental Health Conditions

Approximately twenty percent[1] of our faith-community members and potential participants have a mental health diagnosis. According to the National Alliance on Mental Illness (NAMI) depression is the leading cause of disability worldwide.

According to NAMI:

- Approximately one in five adults in the United States experiences a mental illness in any given year.
- 18.1 percent of adults in the United States experience an anxiety disorder such as post-traumatic stress. disorder, obsessive-compulsive disorder, or specific phobias.
- Generalized anxiety disorder is the most prevalent of all anxiety disorders.
- Among the 20.2 million adults in the U.S. who

experienced a substance use disorder, over 50 percent had a co-occurring mental illness.

Even though most people can be successfully treated, *less than half* of the adults in the U.S. who need services and treatment get the help they need. The average delay between the onset of symptoms and intervention is a shocking eight to ten years.

- Approximately one in five youths from thirteen to eighteen years of age experience a severe mental health condition at some point.
- Thirteen percent of eight to fifteen year olds experience a mental health condition.
- Suicide is the second leading cause of death of youth ages fifteen through twenty-four years old.
- Suicide is the tenth leading cause of death for all Americans.[2]

According to researchers at the Temple University Collaborative on Community Inclusion many people who have a mental health condition regard the connection to one's choice of faith community as one of the important facets of life. Religion and participation in one's faith community strengthens the connection to others and plays a part in recovery.[3]

The Myth of Violence and Mental Health Conditions

Dr. Salzer urges faith communities to address "fears of violence and disruption by people with mental health issues head-on. This is clearly the top thing people are thinking about when they think of inclusion." The myth is that people with mental health issues are violent and unpredictable.

Facts tell a different story. Most people with mental illness are not violent. Only three to five percent of violent acts can be attributed to individuals living with a serious mental illness.[4] People living with a mental health condition are no more prone to violence than anyone else. However, people with severe mental health conditions are over ten times more prone to be victims of violent crime than the general population.

It is incumbent on faith communities to dispel the myth about violence by people with mental health conditions. This belief is what holds people back from talking about their own experiences, let alone disclosing that they are among the twenty percent of people living with a mental health condition.

As faith communities move mental illness from the dark recesses of fear of violence and disruption to the light of belonging and inclusion, people will find a community willing to value and embrace them.

Belonging Counters Stigma

The Reverend Dr. Hollie Holt-Woehl, PhD, devotes her ministry to advancing faith community support and inclusion of people with mental health conditions. Called to this ministry during her Clinical Pastoral Education (CPE) internship, she wrote her doctoral dissertation on congregations and people with mental illness.

The Reverend Dr. Holt-Woehl said, "Stigma follows people with mental health conditions. Many people think, 'I should know better. I should be able to control my own destiny.' Once people share their stories and get supportive responses from their faith communities, it frees them to be who they are."

Many people are reluctant to talk about mental health experiences because of perceived and real concerns of congregational prejudice and discrimination. People are afraid to risk speaking about their experiences. Yet individuals and families often approach clergy and their faith community before seeking other resources or forms of support.

"Belonging is the reason we need to do better," The Reverend Dr. Holt-Woehl said. "Many people I speak with who have a mental health condition tell me 'I feel like I'm the only one. Alone. No one understands."

Leslie Laub is a psychologist and passionate advocate for including people with mental health conditions in faith community life. We have collaborated on faith community inclusion for many years. Leslie encouraged me to broaden my scope to include people with mental health conditions.

Leslie defines stigma *as a sign of disgrace or discredit that sets a person apart*. People with mental health conditions often feel a sense of shame, worthlessness, embarrassment, and self-stigmatization. Some people won't seek medical help, fearing negative responses from people at home, in the community, and at work. People with mental health conditions can encounter discrimination in employment, education, housing, health care, and in the community.

The language we use to describe people who experience mental health conditions can create a healthier environment. Person-first language to talk about someone with a mental health condition emphasizes the individual instead of the diagnosis, for example, "person with schizophrenia" rather than "he's schizophrenic." Avoid generic labels such as "the mentally ill" or judgmental terms like "crazy," lunatic," "insane," "nuts," or "normal," or using words like "suffers from."

In Touch with Personal Feelings

How can congregations become caring communities for people with mental health conditions? It starts with people acknowledging their own experiences with anxiety, depression, fear, paranoia, and uncertainty. The Reverend Dr. Hoelt-Wohl said, "Our fear of supporting people gets us in touch with our own humanness. We are not the masters of our own destiny. We can't control things, other people, or even ourselves. The illusion is we're strong."

Leslie Laub suggests we ask ourselves the following questions to uncover our personal feelings and biases that inadvertently perpetuate prejudice and discrimination. Your answers will help you support someone in a time of crisis, provide a spiritual connection, and allow you to walk alongside them.

- Would you become close friends with a person who has a severe mental health condition?
- Would you encourage your daughter or son to date a person with a severe mental health condition?
- Would you hire a person with a severe mental health condition?
- In your congregation, would you promote and post a policy stating: There will be no discrimination of people related to their race, religion, color, gender, gender expression, age, disability, size, or mental health condition?
- Would you openly encourage your community to invite people with severe mental health conditions to fully participate in services, educational opportunities, committees, and all meetings and festivities?

Create a Caring Community

As a congregation, you must decide to support people with mental health conditions. The Reverend Dr. Hoelt-Wohl said, "Be aware. All of a sudden you will see people who are experiencing a mental health condition, hospitalization, or depression. Or perhaps their child is experiencing eating disorders, psychotic episodes, or changes in behavior. Regardless of the situation or condition, we can see when someone may be suffering or struggling, and needs the support of their faith community. This is the measure of how we care for our people."

The Reverend Dr. Holt-Woehl suggests asking people, "What gives you hope? Ask them what they need. Listen to peoples' stories about their journey with a mental health condition. See the person, and not their condition."

As a faith community, Leslie Laub suggests broadening the scope of your inclusion committee to support people with mental health conditions and then educate your community about mental illness.

Matan Koch is a disability rights advocate and attorney. He speaks to faith-based organizations about the mental health crisis in the United States, and the role they must play to provide support to individuals.

"Faith communities need to understand that inclusion of people with mental health disabilities is a two-sided coin," Matan said, in a personal communication with me. "First, people do not always get the treatment they need, and will have difficulties because of it. Second, the individual's faith community cannot, and should not, focus on solving that, but rather, on meeting the person where they are on any particular day, and providing support so they can participate."

Matan said, "That is inclusion. It may be that the faith community has the resources to help a person solve some of the underlying challenges in their lives. That is an expression of the organization's mission to support its congregants, and is usually done confidentially by clergy and staff. On the day the person shows up at the faith community or an activity, however, they are not a problem to be solved, just a person who wants to participate."

Educate Your Community

The Reverend Dr. Holt-Woehl said, "If you want to educate the congregation, find someone who lives with a mental health condition to share their story. I can preach all day long from the pulpit, but it's not the same as hearing someone tell their story."

When people share their experiences with mental health conditions, it can be powerful. However, Dr. Salzer said, "The research suggests that it is not nearly enough. 'Self-outings' (sharing one's story) may sometimes be harmful to people if the community is not actively working on its own prejudice and discrimination. I believe it will take a huge, concerted, and long-standing effort to promote inclusion, especially of people with serious mental health issues."

You can raise awareness and educate others in a number of ways.

- Talk about mental health conditions. Teach the community there is nothing shameful about having a mental health condition.
- Address prejudice and discrimination in a sermon and in your bulletin. Talk about why we stigmatize people with mental health conditions. Invite the congregation to do soul-searching about why the community

perpetuates stigma, and how it manifests. Share statistics about the frequency of mental health conditions, and how the community can diminish obstacles to participation and support.

- Include the names of people with mental health conditions when your congregation prays for people in need of healing—*if* the individual asks. No one needs to know the reason they are on your prayer list.
- Collaborate with other religious and mental health organizations to sponsor a conference on mental health.
- Give a presentation to the board and staff of your organization. Discuss stigma—what it is, why it exists, and how it affects people in your community. Ask what you can do as a caring community to eliminate prejudice and discrimination.

Often, the obstacle to participation is shame or embarrassment. Explore ways to let people with mental health conditions know that the community is a "Judgment-Free Zone." When people know that yours is a safe community, they may be encouraged to take the first step in the door.

Ask the Person

Chapter 5, "The Spirit of Belonging," is a guide to having conversations with people to build trusting relationships. Listen to people's stories without comment. Ask people:

- How does your mental health condition affect your spirituality?
- What can I do to support you?

Provide Support

The information people share with you can guide you to support them. Compile a list of mental health resources in your community. Contact them for educational resources. Invite one of the organizations to train staff and lay leaders. Invite them to speak at services.

Encourage People to Share Their Gifts and Strengths

A caring community recognizes that people want to belong and engage in faith-community life. Support starts with listening. It includes making sure that people can participate in all the functions of the organization they choose. Participation helps people feel valued and validated as community members. Avoid separate programs and services. Instead work toward supporting and accommodating people with mental health conditions to participate in the same community life with everyone else.

Prepare and Respond to Emergency Situations

The American Psychiatric Association Foundation collaborated with clergy and mental health professionals on an excellent resource, "Mental Health: A Guide for Faith Community Leaders."[5] It includes resources for educating congregations, as well as a section for faith leaders to help support people with mental health conditions.

Be proactive and make sure everyone has gone through training for handling mental health emergencies. Contact your local police department and other first responders to find out if they have a Crisis Intervention Team member available for emergency calls. Ask if they could offer emergency training to your staff. Be sure to discuss what a caller should say when they make a 911 call.

**"Mental Health: A Guide for Faith Community Leaders"
lists three emergency situations that should be addressed
immediately. All clergy and professional staff
should have the phone number readily available to the
closest crisis unit.**

Emergency calls to 911 should be made in these situations.

- If a person poses an immediate danger to himself or others, call 911 right away.

- When a person demonstrates behavior that may be a threat to their safety or that of those around them, call 911. Situations that require calling 911 include:

  o Suicidal behavior;

  o Severe aggressive behavior;

  o Self-mutilation or cutting; or

  o Other self-destructive behavior.

- Suicide. Thoughts of suicide must always be taken seriously. A person may not share these thoughts with you, but family members may be aware of changes in behavior such as giving treasures away, and withdrawing from family and friends. Contemplating suicide is considered a psychiatric emergency and immediate psychiatric evaluation/consultation should be sought. Immediately call 911 for assistance. Ask for a person with the Crisis Intervention Team.

Supporting Parents and Families

Providing family support during a mental health emergency or crisis is one of the most important roles clergy can play. You may be completely comfortable reaching out to parents, but not everyone may be ready for your call. Some will wonder how you learned about their family member; others will just not feel close enough to you to open up and share their fears and feelings. Some parents will see you as a trusted ally during the uncertainty they face. And others will share the story of what happened, share the diagnosis, or ask you to visit their loved one, particularly if they are hospitalized.

Some families have other members who have mental health conditions. Others might warn you not to share any information with professional staff or leaders, fearing the associated stigma, or because the loved one wishes to keep information private. Some family members want to connect with others who have walked this path, or will ask you for additional resources.

Faith can play a compelling role in recovery for both the individual and the family. During these times, keep the door open, call or send an email from time to time, and be ready to embrace them according to their own timeframe.

Food for Thought:
- How are prejudice and discrimination obstacles to belonging for people with mental health conditions and their loved ones?
- What can you do to raise awareness to create a "Judgement-Free" community?

Chapter 22

UNDERSTANDING FAMILIES—THE IMPACT OF DISABILITY

When a child is diagnosed with a disability, parents tumble into an unexpected and uncertain new reality. Not too many parents dream of having a child who has a disability. Dreams of ten fingers and ten toes, the thrill of meeting developmental milestones, and growing up in somewhat predictable ways, often are compromised by such a diagnosis.

– Shelly Christensen

Understanding how parents adapt to raising a child with a disability or mental health condition is at the heart of support for them on this journey. The cornerstone of support that a faith community can provide is based on two things: understanding the needs parents have when a child is diagnosed with a disability, and building a trusting relationship with them.

Faith communities can play a tremendous role to help parents adapt to the challenges they face. You may provide comfort and counseling, or you may open doors to help a child, and his or her family, or engage in religious education and the community.

Author Liane Kupferberg Carter described what it was like raising her son Mickey, who has autism. "Kids like Mickey get left out a lot. They don't get invited to birthday parties, sleepovers, or to play travel soccer. I felt like other families were feasting in a delightful restaurant, while my family stood outside hungry, with our noses pressed against the window. When you feel isolated like that, the one place you naturally look to is your faith community, but when Mickey was a boy, many schools and synagogues just didn't get it. They were turning away families from early childhood programs, and Hebrew schools, and summer camps, because they weren't equipped to help. It wasn't done out of malice. It was done out of ignorance."[1]

"Why Me? Why My Child?"

Parents adapt to the challenges of raising a child with a disability in diverse ways. Learning how parents and families navigate this journey will help you understand the complexities they face.

The diagnosis shakes parents deeply. The dreams we have for our child disappear amidst the shock and uncertainly of the diagnosis. Some of us resist our new reality, adapting slowly, uncertainly, and unwillingly. We are devastated by the sense of isolation and think no one else has ever gone through this. We feel powerless, for it seems that all control over the child's life is shifted to doctors, special educators, and social workers. For most parents this is a journey not chosen.

Parents may be immobilized by fear for the child's future, and feel overwhelmed as they realize they don't even know where to begin. Parents may deny their child's developmental differences, even with a diagnosis. Denial is purposeful. It gives parents time to come to terms with the diagnosis. Some parents are concerned the child will not be able to participate in their faith community's activities such as preschool, religious school, or life-cycle events.

Parents Have Needs

It is difficult for parents to recognize their own needs when consumed with caring for their child with a disability. Their needs for information, social support, emotional support, and making meaning out of a difficult situation, are the very things that help parents navigate their journey.

These are the four needs that parents have:

• **Information.** What is the diagnosis? What does it mean for my child? What services are available, and who can provide them? Is there anyone else who has been through this who can tell me what to do first? Who can I trust?

There is an overwhelming amount of information available. Yet it is not surprising when parents struggle to make it from one day to the next. They process information, search for medical providers, and schedule appointments—often while juggling the rest of life, such as work and family. Gathering information is time consuming and confusing. It is helpful for a parent to speak to other parents whose children have similar disabilities, and who can share information from their own experiences.

• **Social Support.** When a child is diagnosed, the sense of isolation profoundly impacts parents. Parents often feel they are alone. Family and friends may not understand the new and vast set of changes and challenges. Extended family members, traditionally a source of support, may not be nearby to provide comfort, or may be experiencing their own grief. Friends who have children with typical development may not understand. Just the presence of those friends can be too painful for a parent of a newly diagnosed child.

Because of the potentially overwhelming responsibilities of caring for the child, parents may not have the time or energy to pick up the phone and call a friend. Parents often report that their circle of friends changes throughout this journey as they seek out others with similar experiences. Social isolation can be devastating, and parents must find ways to connect to others whom they can trust.

• **Emotional Support.** Emotions play a significant role against the backdrop of disability, and include anger, denial, and depression. Parents may bargain with a higher power to fix the disability. When bargaining doesn't seem to help and emotions are overwhelming, parents may experience depression. If emotions impair daily functioning, parents should seek professional help. This may help them make meaning of the journey, and adapt to the role of a parent of a child with a disability.

• **Making Meaning.** As parents seek to find ways to deal with their unplanned journey, they often ask, "Why me?" When the question is unanswered, parents can change the nature of their thinking. Instead of looking outside of themselves for answers, they begin to reflect on their role as the parent of a child with a disability. Making meaning of the journey does not mean knowing why this has happened. It means parents know they will take each day as it comes. Although there will be potholes and detours on the journey many others have been down this road before.

Making meaning signifies that a parent is adapting to the role of raising their child.

The Evolution

In time, some parents will begin to see their child's diagnosis as an opportunity rather than a disruption. Elaine Hall described how she approached raising her autistic son Neal in *Now I See the Moon.*

In a personal communication, Elaine said that she began entering into her child's autistic world so she could see the world from his perspective. She figured if he wasn't comfortable in the 'normal' ways of things, she would see what interested him.

Elaine said, "When he would spin in circles, I would spin with him making it Ring-Around-the-Rosie. When he would stare at his hand, I would too, and noticed the miraculous way the hand opens and closes, grasps and releases." What began as a mother trying desperately to connect with her son, turned into a shared experience.

This upheaval in Elaine's life, when Neal was diagnosed with autism, turned into her life's mission. Elaine used the same methods she used with Neal to create The Miracle Project, a fully inclusive theatre, film, and religious education program profiled in the two-time Emmy Award winning film, "Autism: The Musical." Neal, now a young adult, speaks using a communication device, shares his journey with faith communities, and has given a presentation at the United Nations.

The evolution of a parent with a child with a disability as a series of stages resonated with me. It's a refreshing and non-judgmental perspective on how parents grow and adapt. When I turned this lens on my own journey, I felt empowered. I realized what I was experiencing was not unusual, or eternally full of despair. Dr. Nancy Miller, a social worker and anthropologist, identified the four "Stages of Adaptation" to describe the process: Surviving, Searching, Settling In, and Separating.[2] These are stages that many parents experience raising children with disabilities. I learned that with each transition in my child's life, I return to surviving as I adapt to new experiences.

• **Surviving** includes reacting and coping. In this stage, parents experience helplessness when they begin to realize that something completely out of their control has taken away their child's equal chance at life. It involves uncomfortable feelings including fear, confusion, guilt, blame, shame, and anger. Parents navigate and survive by understanding that many others share the feelings they are experiencing. Many parents remember a specific event, or point in time, when they started to regain control, optimism, and hope. Parents begin to feel a sense of purpose and confidence as they start moving ahead with life.

• **Searching** includes both an *outer search* and an *inner search*. The outer search begins in the surviving stage. Searching for information about the diagnosis, how it impacts the child, and where to find services and support is an overwhelming process. Inner searching occurs when parents begin to reframe their identity as the parent of a child with a disability. Inner searching involves the quest for understanding personal and societal attitudes about disability. Parents' priorities shift, and relationships with friends and family can change. In their inner search parents can feel incompetent, frightened, and overwhelmed, while others feel motivated, needed, and fulfilled as they embrace the challenges that lie ahead.

• **Settling In** is characterized by the beginning of treatment programs, special education and other interventions. Outer searching has subsided for a while. Parents realize that change takes time, and their other children need them. They settle into a "new normal." In this stage, parents are armed with information, skills, confidence, and assertiveness. They have established a support network and can access resources.

• **Separating** begins at birth. It is a gradual process that occurs in small steps for all parents and children. When a child has a disability, the process may be altered or slowed down. Some children may not initiate separating experiences, and parents may need different or additional support to help children become more independent and self-sufficient. A parent's self-worth and self-esteem are often intertwined with their child's daily life. It can be difficult to step back and possibly see their child struggle. Separating brings back feelings from the surviving stage, such as guilt, grieving, and psychological turmoil. It involves the return to both outer and inner searching to reach the new level of settling in.

How Are Siblings Affected?

How does the disability affect the siblings? The experience can be positive and enriching. Some siblings become involved in helping parents care for the sibling with a disability, often assuming responsibilities beyond their years. Siblings can become ardent supporters and protectors of their brother or sister, feeling pride as their sibling makes gains in learning or development. In contrast, some siblings feel bitterness, resentment, and anger toward both their parents and their brother or sister with a disability. They may feel jealous, neglected, and rejected as they see their parents' energy, attention, money, and psychological support flow away from them.

Ages and developmental levels play a role in the reaction and adjustment of siblings. A younger sibling without a disability may not understand the situation or be able to interpret events realistically. He may be confused about the disability, think he is to blame, or even be worried that he will catch the disability. Older children worry about the future of their sibling, how their own peers will react, and whether they will pass the disability on to their own children.

As parents we want to treat each child fairly. Siblings may be tuned in to how parents show their love and approval, especially when they see or feel that their parents pay more attention to the child with a disability. It's important for parents to recognize that they need to ask for help so they can spend more time with other children. Giving their other children the time, attention, and love they need can ease siblings concerns and strengthen the family.

Having a child with a disability is part of the fabric that makes families unique. The impact all children in the family have, along with parenting styles and the interactions between family members, are the things that create a family. Parents love, respect, disagree, and work together to give their children the quality of life they dreamed of from the day each child was born. It can be difficult adapting to the changing conditions involved with raising a child with a disability. Seeking information, learning as much as possible about the disability, honoring all our children's considerable strengths, and supporting our own hopes and dreams for them can be life affirming.

Ask Parents to Tell You Their Story

Clergy can be a source of wisdom and caring. Clergy can help parents talk through their concerns in a caring environment to gain a clearer perspective on living with a child with a disability. Fears of the future can immobilize the needs of today, so it is important to help parents stay focused on the reality of the moment. Worrying about the future depletes the energy needed for the present, and may even cloud the small positive things that happen every day.

Some parents benefit from counseling. Counseling can often help them become aware of the many changes they and their families are going through. Counseling can help parents understand their own feelings and help them adapt to a "new normal" in their lives. Because parents' emotions and needs ebb and flow throughout the child's lifespan, they may need to return to counseling *at various transition points.*

Understanding the parents' journey is valuable to parents and professionals alike. Parents must eventually come to terms with ambiguous loss as they seek to find hope for the future. If parents do not go through the process, they often become stuck in denying the reality. For some, this is manifested in anger toward God, medical and educational professionals, and sometimes, even toward the child with the disability. This is where a trusted member of the clergy can support parents, providing a stable and nurturing backdrop as they travel this often isolating road back to hope.

Partnering with Parents

- Be an ally. Parents need reliable allies in this journey, someone who embodies the qualities of empathy, commitment, and trustworthiness. Reliable allies focus on supporting both the family and the child to achieve success.

- Successful partnerships depend on collaboration. Encourage parents to talk about their child. It helps them share their hopes and dreams. The can talk about the challenges and strengths of their child. Remember, collaboration results in each person in the partnership sharing knowledge and working together to create a plan of action. Think of this alliance as creating a whole that is much greater than the sum of its parts.

- Build trust. Parents expend a lot of time and energy advocating for their child. Some parents, skeptical of professionals, find it hard to build trust. Without trust, it is difficult to work together. Trust is based on the willingness to try new things and recognize if it is time to make changes. Be patient.

- Avoid power struggles. When one party holds the power

over another, even unintentionally, any attempt at collaboration is doomed to fail. If holding power over one another is the objective, rather than having open communication about meeting the child's needs, the child is the one who loses.

As a caring professional, guard against wanting to "fix" the child or the parents, or find solutions based on minimal information or input. There is nothing to fix. But there are many opportunities to welcome a child and the family by getting to know them, understanding parents' hopes and dreams for their child, and working together. In order to really support the child and family, do not expect to have short hallway conversations or quick cookie-cutter conferences. Listening, understanding, and building a trusting relationship between partners will nurture a strong and healthy collaboration.

Collaboration was something Karen Jackson hoped to find in her faith community. Karen is the Founder and Executive Director of Faith Inclusion Network of Hampton Roads in Virginia, and the author of *Loving Samantha.* In a personal communication to me, Karen shared her family's experiences with her congregation. "At nine years old, my daughter Samantha exhibited some very challenging autistic behaviors, including the inability to sit still for even five minutes, loud vocalizations, and tantrums. I knew that if our *whole* family was going to be part of a faith community, we would need a lot of support and understanding. I had no idea what that support would look like, but I had gotten to a point that I could not let my three children, including Samantha, grow up without learning about their faith and being part of a con-gregation."

Karen continued, "I will never forget meeting with the director of religious education as new parishioners at Blessed

Sacrament Catholic Church in Norfolk, Virginia. After explaining the situation, Sister Regina responded, 'We don't know much about autism, but together we can figure out how to include Samantha.' Acceptance and a willingness to include—that is what our church gave to us then, and why we still attend today."

Food for Thought:
- What did you learn about the needs parents have when a child is diagnosed?
- Think about a family you have worked with. After reading this chapter, what would you change about how you support them?

Chapter 23

SUPPORTING PEOPLE IN DIFFICULT TIMES

By day, the Lord will command God's loving kindness
And at night, God's resting place will be with me;
This is my prayer to the Almighty, God of my life.

— Psalm 42:9

Jack's Story

Jack, an 86-year-old Jewish man with intellectual disabilities, lived in a group home. Mary, the supervisor of the home, asked me for help finding where his parents were buried. Jack wanted to be buried near them but couldn't remember their first names. Identifying, preserving, and facilitating Jack's end-of-life decisions became a joint partnership between his support staff and his faith community.

Jack was twelve years old when he was removed from his family home and placed in a state institution for people with disabilities. In those days, doctors and clergy often counseled parents to place children with disabilities in an institution—and then forget about them. In the 1980's, Jack left the institution where he resided for over fifty years, and went to live in a group home with three other men with disabilities.

Advocating for Jack, Mary found his parents' names in

an old file. I called the funeral home and gave them Jack's parents' names. They checked their records and found the location of the graves. That same day Mary took Jack to the cemetery to visit his parent's graves. It was a deeply emotional and significant experience for Jack. Ironically, his parents' graves were less than two miles from his home.

Jack was very connected to his Jewish roots even though he hadn't been part of the community for nearly seventy-five years. Jack deeply desired to be buried in his faith tradition. I wondered about his life before the institution, how he maintained his identity as a Jew, and if he had expressed his religious and spiritual wishes at any time before now.

A year after visiting his parents' graves, Mary told me that Jack was in the hospital and not expected to live. I made a call to arrange for a rabbi to visit Jack in the hospital and to recite the traditional "*Viddui*," a prayer of confession recited before one's death.

Mary called again a few days later to tell me Jack had died. The graveside funeral was officiated by a rabbi who had once visited Jack in the state residential facility. According to Jack's wishes, he was buried near his parents.

After the funeral, the mourners went to Jack's home for the traditional meal of consolation. Many synagogues read Jack's name during *Sheloshim,* the thirty-day period of mourning. The Jewish press printed his obituary. The community helped pay additional funeral costs. Without this assistance, Jack would not have been able to be buried according to Jewish ritual.

The community came together to support Jack. I wondered how Jack's life would have changed had he been included in his faith community during his life. Sadly, we will never know.

Grace's Story

Grace was intent on finding a congregation she could call "home." Her search, which was supported by her direct support professionals, was fruitful, and she started attending services at her new congregation. Grace, who lived with an intellectual disability, sang in the choir, and was a regular at weekly Bible study. Everyone knew her by name, and she was never at a loss for dinner invitations and rides. In fact, one of her greatest joys was to invite her fellow congregants to her house.

Grace died unexpectedly. Her funeral was held in her faith community. Many people attended her funeral and the burial. That evening her family invited friends from Grace's congregation to her home to share their favorite stories about Grace. It was clear how much she was loved, and how much she would be missed.

So often society regards people with disabilities and mental health conditions as people who are recipients—*rather than as people who have much to share in faith community life.* As faith-based organizations, we can change that starting now, so another Jack doesn't have to live separate from a community that is important to him—while another Grace is recognized as a valued and important contributor.

We all just want to belong.

Supporting People with Disabilities When a Loved One Dies

People with disabilities need comfort and support in bereavement like anyone else.

The commonly held belief that people with disabilities don't understand death, or don't mourn may leave them without the tools they need to process grief and loss. Adults with disabilities have thoughts and feelings around grief and loss like anyone else. Helping people with intellectual and developmental disabilities find their voice may be different but just as critical.

How can your faith community support a person with a disability when a family member, friend, or caregiver dies?

The Vanderbilt Kennedy Center on Excellence in Developmental Disabilities recommends giving accurate and honest information to people with disabilities and providing them with individualized support to process grief.[1] Trying to protect people from feelings of mourning can prolong bereavement. Anxiety or depression may occur. Use straightforward explanations, not euphemisms, such as "Grandfather went to sleep," which may stir up fears that going to sleep causes death.

Family members with disabilities can share memories for the eulogy and participate in funeral rituals which help them understand that someone important to them has died. If the person with a disability has someone outside of the immediate family they trust, ask that individual to offer support during the funeral and burial services.

People with disabilities may need more concrete rituals, explicit directions, and simplified activities. People who are non-speaking, or who don't have the vocabulary to express their feelings and thoughts, may express them through behavior.

In the days and months following the death, encourage people to look at photographs, tell stories, and share memories about their loved one.

The loss of presence in everyday life is a concrete reminder of a person's death for mourners. Every family member experiences bold reminders when routines such as daily phone calls or regular dinners together are gone. People with disabilities are not just the recipients of support and comfort—they can also give support to those who love them.

Supporting Children with Disabilities When a Loved One Dies

Although children with disabilities may express feelings differently from their siblings and peers without disabilities, the grief is just as authentic. Children may repeat the same questions as they try to understand death and process their feelings. Be patient. Encourage them to talk about the person and the things they did together. Include them when the family gathers so they begin to understand that other people feel sad, too.

Meredith Polsky and Arlen Grad Gaines wrote *I Have A Question About Death: A Book for Children with Autism Spectrum Disorders or Other Special Needs.*[2] The authors knew that parents and clergy often avoided talking about death with children with disabilities. Meredith said, "Avoiding the subject leads to even more confusion and fear. We wanted to fill this gap in children's literature to assist parents, educators, and caregivers approach the topic of death with any child, and help families navigate loss in their own lives."

Meredith and Arlen offer the following strategies to help children when a loved one dies.

- Use direct language. Euphemisms such as "passed away," "went to sleep," or "in a better place," are confusing for children. Use the word "died."
- Talk to children about the emotions they may feel. Some people might cry because they are sad, or laugh because they are remembering a funny story. Assure children that people respond differently, and that anything they feel is okay.
- Explain what to expect at the funeral and other gatherings of mourners. There may be a lot of people around when someone dies. There might be a lot of noise. People might want to hug them. People say they are sorry when what they really mean is that they are sad.
- Utilize strategies that have been helpful for the child in other situations. For example, bring along a comforting toy, and find a quiet place the child can go if they need a break.
- Maintain structure and routine for the child to minimize transitions and disruptions.

Supporting Children with Disabilities When a Family Pet Dies

Before my family began adopting rescue dogs, our kids had hamsters. Jacob had a knack for caring for these little escape artists, and his hamsters lived unusually long lives. His first hamster, Tyke, was around six years old when he died. Jacob prepared his body for burial in our yard under the lilac tree, putting him in a small box stuffed with cotton, and sealing it with a ribbon. We held a funeral for Tyke, and it seemed to help us all feel a little better.

Later that evening, I knocked on Jacob's door. He was

sitting on the floor cleaning out Tyke's cage. I thought how sad he must be feeling, and said, "Jacob, I'm so sorry about Tyke."

He turned around and looked puzzled. "Mom, why are you saying you're sorry? You didn't do anything!"

I realized then that the words of comfort we say to someone who is grieving are almost by rote. Jacob gave me pause. To him, the words "I'm sorry" are what you say when you apologize for something you've done, and not as an expression of sympathy. Typical expressions of sympathy may not have meaning for some children. Jacob and I talked about Tyke's life, the ways Jacob cared for him, and about feeling sad that he died.

When a family pet dies, children can feel the loss deeply. The absence of food and water bowls are reminders of the loss. Ask children to share their memories and photographs. If the family gets another pet, talk about how the new pet does not replace the one that died. Ask if your faith community has resources for the loss of a pet, or create your own.

My family continued to adopt hamsters while the kids were still young until Jaime came along. Jaime was our first dog. She was a six-month-old, forty-pound black and white rescue dog, and we all fell in love with her. Jaime lived to be nearly twelve when she was diagnosed with a brain tumor. With reluctance and sadness our family made the decision to euthanize Jaime. We stayed with her while the veterinarian administered the drugs.

We all mourned the death of our beautiful Jaime. Through my tears I explained our sadness to our three sons, "We loved Jaime so much, and she loved us back. If we hadn't loved her so much, it wouldn't hurt so much now." Sharing our grief, talking about our feelings, and sharing our memories of Jaime with each other gave us comfort. We walked through this journey of loss as a family.

Food for Thought:
- What are some euphemisms we tend to use when talking about the death of someone in our family or community? What are more direct ways to talk about death?
- What are some traditions your family or faith community has surrounding the death of a pet? What new traditions might be comforting or helpful?

Chapter 24

OPEN THE DOOR TO A NEW DAY

*Sing out to God a new song, praise the Holy One
wherever the faithful gather.*

-Psalm 149

Including people with disabilities in faith community life *is not a new concept*. Inclusion is substantiated as a moral mandate based on the values that we embrace as people of faith. We are commanded *not* to place stumbling blocks before people, but often we are oblivious to the obstacles that shut people out, or limit participation.

A faith community becomes richer when all pathways are open so each person can share their gifts, talents, and strengths.

Each of us has our own perspective and understanding of belonging and inclusion. To me it is a culture that welcomes, accepts, and embraces all people.

When I close my eyes and imagine inclusion as a priority, I see:
- People participating in the faith community they choose.
- A place where people with disabilities and mental health conditions can contribute their gifts and strengths, and where relationships are formed based on common interests.
- Faith communities walking alongside people, comforting them, encouraging them, and supporting them on their way to belonging.

- Children with disabilities in classrooms, playgrounds, and camp bunks with their peers.
- Teens actively involved in the activities of their youth group.
- Adults worshipping, volunteering, teaching, preaching, and going on missions where people are in need.
- Marriages and children and life-cycle events.
- Each one of us recognizing the spark of the Divine in each person we meet.

What is *your* vision of belonging and inclusion?

Rabbi Lynne Landsberg, in one of our many conversations, shared her thoughts about a teaching from the Talmud. *Rabbi Yohanan said: One may only pray in a house with windows (Berachot 34B).*

The reason our sanctuaries and prayer spaces have windows, Rabbi Landsberg observed, was so every person inside a house of prayer could look out and see who was waiting to come in.

It's time to open those doors in joy and celebration so all people can belong!

ACKNOWLEDGMENTS

I am deeply grateful and blessed to have discovered my life's work. The journey is so much richer because of the people I've met and shared it with. No one does this alone!

Rabbi Lynne Landsberg, to whom this book is dedicated, died on February 26, 2018. She and I became friends for so many reasons—our work in the Reform Jewish movement, our passion for justice, our love of thrift shopping, and our love for the Law and Order-SVU TV show. Lynne encouraged me, challenged me, and went to bat for me. Everyone needs a "Lynne" in their lives.

In *Pirke Avot,* Ben Zoma says, "Who is wise? He who learns from everyone." My wisdom grows daily because of so many people whose lives have intersected with mine.

Sharon Palay, who has taught me the meaning of belonging, Paula Fox, of blessed memory, for our memorable car conversations and her wisdom, and Bob Kusnetz, who inspired the title of this book.

Ginny Thornburgh, Becca Hornstein, the Rev. Bill Gaventa, Steve Eidelman, and Nancy Weiss, all mentors who showed me the way and supported my leadership journey. Your words and your guidance continue to shape my work.

Jay and Shira Ruderman and the team at the Ruderman Family Foundation, thank you for your philanthropic support, leadership, and commitment to disability inclusion. You have been there every step of the way for many of the initiatives I'm honored to be involved with.

Anne Masters, David Morstad, Dr. Neil Cudney, and Dr.

Debby Fisher, my colleagues on the leadership team of the Religion and Spirituality Interest Network of AAIDD, who always share their friendship, knowledge, and encouragement with a hearty dose of laughter.

Rabbi Edie Menscher and Rabbi Richard Address for inviting me in to share my work with the Union for Reform Judaism. I am proud of the body of work we started and advanced through the years.

Sarah Kranz Ciment, Chaya Perman, Marcy Horwitz, Chani Baram, and Rabbi Shmaya Krinsky of the Ruderman Chabad Inclusion Initiative for inviting me to join the team, introducing me to The Lubavitcher Rebbe, and caring for me through joys and sorrows.

Ed Frim of the United Synagogue of Conservative Judaism, for your good counsel and the opportunity to work with the inclusion cohorts.

Batya Jacob of Yachad at the Orthodox Union, for years of friendship, collaboration, and guidance on grandparenting twins.

Dr. Mark Salzer, Liane Kupferberg Carter, Meredith Polsky, Elaine Hall, Neal Katz, Dr. Stephen Shore, Rev. Hollie Holt-Woehl, Leslie Laub, Matan Koch, Sheryl Grossman, Michelle Steinhart, Lisa Friedman, Dr. Shana Erenberg, Dr. Sara Rubinow Simon, Dr. Erik Carter, Jennifer Bumble, Becky Henry, Lisa Handelman, Gabrielle Kaplan-Mayer, Liz Weintraub, Karen Jackson, Liv Mendelsohn, Rebecca Wanatick, Sherry Grossman, Ellen Maiseloff, Arlene Remz, Helen Winoker, Rachel Turniansky, Sandy Miller-Jacobs, Jodi Newmark, Caitlin Bailey, Lisa Jamieson, Kristen Loomis for all the conversations, collaborations, and sharing innovative practices with me.

Kay McCullum, Margie Earhart, Jan Frisch, Linda Krueger, Debby Joseph, and Lauri Meyers. Your beta reading of the earlier versions of *From Longing to Belonging* provided the candid feedback that shaped the final version.

Connie Anderson, my editor at Words and Deeds, and Ann Aubitz, my publishing guru at FuzionPrint. I am so grateful that I found Women of Words (WOW)—and the two of you. You taught me to be an author. And to all of the WOW sisters…thank you all for sharing your writing and publishing experiences and your encouragement, keeping me afloat time and again. Diane Keynes, I'm grateful for your fresh set of eyes and perspective.

Rabbis Norman Cohen, David Locketz, Jill Crimmings, and Cantor Sarah Lipsett-Allison, of blessed memory, for making Bet Shalom the inclusive congregation it is for so many of us.

I stand on the shoulders of those who have gone before me. My parents, Paul and Shirley Thomas, my grandparents, Ann and Max Horn, and Celia and Ralph Thomas, my aunt Florence Winner, and my best friend Carla Meyers. They taught me to soar with my strengths and to laugh in all the right places. May their memories be for blessing.

My family is my inspiration. My husband Rick Christensen whose love is the foundation of my life; our sons, Aaron, Jacob, and Zachary, and daughter-in-law, Nancy, who give their "Little Mom" pride and happiness; our grandchildren, Eli, Isaac, Anna, and Eve, who give their Bubie and Zadie (Grandma and Grandpa, in Yiddish) the gifts of joy and wonder; my brother Ralph, who I admire for his tenacity and creativity; my aunt, Elaine Greenberg, the little "*shvester*," who can always make lemonade out of lemons; and Margie Earhart, the Ethel Mertz to my Lucy Ricardo.

Finally, I thank God for all the blessings in my life.

ABOUT THE AUTHOR

Shelly Christensen, MA, did not intend to be an award-winning consultant, speaker, and author in the faith community disability inclusion field. As a budding writer, she penned her first play in fifth grade about an arson investigation, and was the editorial page editor and writer for her high school newspaper, *The Robin's Tale*. She earned her Bachelor of Arts degree in journalism, which appealed to her because there were no math prerequisites.

Shelly's life took a decidedly different turn when her son, Jacob, was diagnosed with attention deficit hyperactivity disorder and eventually with Asperger syndrome. This mother did the only thing she knew she could do. She met the challenges of public school education with an intuitive passion, often saying, "Children have one crack at an education, and no one is going to take that away from my kid!" After an initial stint as a headstrong and demanding parent, which didn't work too well on her son's behalf, Shelly learned the art of collaboration, advocacy, and respect to build a strong parent-school relationship. She was the kind of parent special education professionals love to have on their team.

Shelly directed the Jewish Community Inclusion Program for People with Disabilities at Jewish Family and Children's Service of Minneapolis for thirteen years. The same passion that guided her as a parent was the impetus for innovation as she led Jewish community organizations to move toward inclusion and acceptance of people with disabilities and their loved ones.

Shelly is a leader in the growing faith community disability inclusion movement. She is an international speaker and consultant to numerous faith communities, faith-based organizations, and disability organizations.

Shelly and her husband Rick live in Minneapolis, Minnesota with their Shelties, Penina and Caleb.

APPENDICES

Appendix A
The Americans with Disabilities Act – A Moral Mandate
What does the Lord require of you but to do justice,
and to love kindness, and
to walk humbly with your God.

-Micah 6:8

The Americans with Disabilities Act, (ADA), signed into law by President George H.W. Bush in 1990, is the most comprehensive federal civil-rights statute protecting the rights of people with disabilities, entitling over fifty-six million Americans to equal opportunities as full citizens of the United States. The ADA affects employment; federal, state and local government programs and services; and access to places of public accommodation such as businesses, transportation, and non-profit service providers. The ADA's civil rights protections are parallel to those that have previously been established by the federal government for women, racial, ethnic and religious minorities.

An individual is protected under the ADA if he or she is an individual with a disability who:

1) has a physical or mental impairment that substantially limits one or more life activities; or

2) has a record of such an impairment; or

3) is regarded as having such an impairment. [1]

Further, the person must be qualified for the program, service or job. The ADA protections incorporate "major life activities"

292 - Shelly Christensen

including, but not limited to, caring for oneself, performing manual tasks, seeing, hearing, eating, sleeping, walking, standing, lifting, bending, speaking, breathing, learning, reading, concentrating, thinking, communicating and working.[2]

Title I: Employment and Religious Organizations

Title I of the ADA covers employment of people with disabilities. The regulations guide employers with instructions on hiring and promoting people with disabilities.

1. Employers may not discriminate against an individual with a disability in any aspect of the employment process, including hiring or promotion, if the person is otherwise qualified for the job.

2. The ADA prohibits pre-employment inquiries about a disability, requiring that such inquiries be made in the post-offer stage of the hiring process. Before making a job offer, an employer:

    •   May ask questions about an applicant's ability to perform specific job functions

    •   May not ask about a disability

    •   May make a job offer that is conditioned on satisfactory results of a post-offer medical examination or inquiry.

    During the initial interview process, leading questions seeking information about a possible disabling condition should be avoided. Interviewers may ask any number of questions related to the essential functions of the job and the applicant's ability to perform such tasks.

3. When asked, employers must provide a reasonable accommodation to the known disability of qualified

individuals. This includes job restructuring and modification of equipment.

4. Employers do not need to provide accommodations that impose an undue hardship on operations. They do, however, need to determine the difficulty or cost of accommodations before attempting to establish an undue hardship defense. *Undue hardship* is defined as an action requiring significant difficulty or expense when considered in light of factors such as an employer's size, financial resources, and the nature and structure of its operation.

5. A religious organization may give preference in the hiring process to an individual of a particular religion to perform work connected with its activities. For example, hiring of clergy is not covered under Title I.

6. Religious organizations with fifteen or more employees are responsible for compliance with Title I.

7. Job descriptions should be based on the essential functions required to perform adequately in a given job. Such functional descriptions encourage a reliable comparison between the needs of the organization and the qualifications of the applicant.

8. An employer is not required to lower quality or production standards to make an accommodation, nor is an employer obligated to provide personal use items such as glasses or hearing aids.

An accommodation is any modification or adjustment to a job, work environment, or the way things are usually done, that enables a qualified individual with a disability to enjoy an equal employment opportunity. Just because a person has a disability or limitation does not mean he or she will require workplace accommodations. An individual may have a disability that does not necessarily limit the ability to perform job functions. Each accommodation process is handled on a case-by-case basis to ensure the needs of the specific individual are met.

Title II: Religious Communities and Public Services
Public Transportation

Public transportation can be a concern for faith communities. One of the obstacles to participation is not having transportation to existing programs and services. The ADA mandates that public transit buses must be accessible to individuals with disabilities. Transit authorities must provide comparable paratransit or other special transportation services to individuals with disabilities who cannot use fixed route bus services.

If public transportation services are not available, how will people who need rides find their way? Many congregations have transportation committees that coordinate volunteers to drive people to events. Others have a transportation fund to help pay for taxis and rideshare options.

Public Services and Religious Communities

A religious organization may be covered under Title II if it participates in a state or local government program that provides services to the public, such as meal sites or counseling centers. Since the state or local government is obligated to comply with the ADA, and other applicable non-discrimination legislation, a religious organization, by virtue of its participation in the program, may not discriminate against individuals with disabilities in the provision of contracted services.

Title III: Religious Communities and Public Accommodations

Title III does not apply to religious organizations or entities controlled by religious organizations including places of worship. Generally, worship space, social halls, religious schools, and residences for clergy would be exempt under Title III.

However, if a faith community leases space to a public accommodation, the public accommodation (e.g., the tenant) must ensure the space it leases meets the requirements of Title III. For example, if your congregation leases space to a separate organization, such as a daycare or a company for meetings, then you must comply under Title III.

Faith communities can reference Title III when evaluating organizational policies and practices. For example, public accommodations must allow service animals to accompany an individual, because the animal is an accommodation, allowing that person access to participation.

- People with disabilities must be accorded full and equal enjoyment of the goods and services of a place of public accommodation.
- It is discriminatory not to allow people with disabilities to have the full and equal enjoyment of any public accommodation.
- Eligibility criteria that screen out, or tend to screen out, people with disabilities are prohibited.
- Public accommodations are required to make reasonable modifications in policies, practices, and procedures whenever it is necessary to provide services to a person with a disability, unless the modification would fundamentally alter the nature of the service

provided.
- Auxiliary aids and services must be provided to individuals with disabilities unless an undue burden would result to the public accommodation.
- All new construction and alterations of facilities must be accessible. **

** Use the ADA as a guide if you are planning new construction or renovations of facilities.

The ADA is landmark legislation for many people who, prior to its passage, couldn't even cross the street while using a wheelchair, use the restrooms in public buildings or ride public transportation. It is a model to follow, a moral mandate, that enforces the freedom to be an equal and valued member of one's faith community.

Appendix B
Accessibility Statements and Accommodation Requests

We all do better when we all do better.
-Sen. Paul Wellstone

An accessibility statement should be standard in *all* electronic and written publications, registration forms, invitations, and websites. It clearly states that your organization welcomes people with disabilities, including to services, classes, events, meetings, and programs. An accessibility statement can be as simple as:

"We are an inclusive organization, and welcome all."

Or, if you want to be more specific:

"We are committed to working towards full participation and accessibility for people with disabilities and mental health conditions."

Accommodation requests invite individuals to tell you about their needs in order to participate. Always include contact information and a due date for requests to be made. The following statements invite people to contact the organization with their requests:

"If you require an accommodation in order to participate in (the meeting/services/event, etc.) please contact _____ (name of individual who is responsible to take requests, if applicable) at (phone number) or email (address) by (due date to make the request)."

"We welcome and support children, teens, and adults with disabilities, mental health conditions, and their families. We make every effort to ensure our programs, equipment, and facilities are accessible to all. Please phone xxx-xxx-xxxx or email (address) if you have any questions, or would like to request an accommodation."

Additional language may be added to state that requests for accommodations that are made after the advertised date everything possible will be done to honor them.

People often ask if an American Sign Language (ASL) interpreter should be provided at an event, even if no requests have been made. If the organization has included an accommodation statement and no requests have been made, it is reasonable not have an interpreter. Some organizations hire interpreters even if no requests have been made.

Inform people that meeting and conference facilities are accessible with a simple statement: The facility is accessible to individuals with disabilities.

Appendix C
Event Planning Checklist

Events and programs should be accessible to all who wish to participate. The Event Planning Checklist is useful for every step starting with finding an accessible location through the actual event or program. The checklist is also included in the **Companion Workbook**.

Location of Your Event

Consider how easily accessible your event will be. This checklist will help you evaluate possible locations:

- ☐ Is accessible parking located near the building entrance?

- ☐ Is there access from the curb to the entrance for participants who are dropped off or use accessible transportation?

- ☐ Does the auditorium have good visibility for those who use a wheelchair? Are there places for those who use a wheelchair to sit with family and friends?

- ☐ Are accessible restrooms convenient to the areas you will be using?

- ☐ How many accessible restrooms or stalls are available?

- ☐ Is there ample room in the dining room for someone using a wheelchair to pass between tables?

- ☐ Does the facility offer assistive listening technology?

- ☐ Does the facility provide good quality lighting?

- ☐ Are elevators convenient to building and event room

entrances?

☐ Do you require other accommodations, such as a ramp to the stage? If so, how much will this cost?

☐ Are coatrooms accessible and located near accessible entrances? If not, can a coat rack be positioned near entrances?

☐ Does the venue have a safety plan to evacuate people who require assistance? Ask to review the plan, and share with your event team.

For more information on the responsibility of hotels and other rented facilities, contact your state or regional ADA office or visit Information and Technical Assistance on the ADA homepage.[1]

Marketing Your Event

- When you invite people to any program, event, or service, include an accessibility statement on the invitation or announcement. See Appendix B for examples of accessibility statements.

- Include a due date to request accommodations so you have enough time to make the arrangements.

- Include the start and end times of your event so people who use paratransit can reserve transportation to and from the event.

- The cost to attend an event is often an obstacle for some people. People may be embarrassed to ask for a reduced or waived fee. Add language to encourage them to contact you. "All participants are welcome. Requests for fee arrangements are confidential. Please contact (name, phone, email) to discuss your needs."

The person who handles these requests should be a member of the professional staff.

Event Planning

- Ask people with disabilities and mental health conditions to participate in all aspects of event planning, not just those that pertain to inclusion. Volunteering is a significant point of entry for many people, and provides an opportunity to contribute.
- Understand that transportation may prove to be a barrier to participation. Explore the possibility of providing volunteer transportation or creating a fund to pay for accessible transportation.
- If someone who uses a wheelchair or other mobility device will be called to the stage, make sure the venue has a permanent ramp, lift, or will provide a portable ramp.

At Your Event

- Arrive early to make sure all accommodations have been made at the venue.
- Place the registration table in an accessible location.
- Check accessible routes to tables so someone who uses a wheelchair can pass by without any obstacles.
- Make sure assistive listening technology is available and working.
- Have large-print materials and Braille materials available at the registration desk.
- Reserve space for participants who require sign language interpretation at the front of the room.

- Check with your meeting planner or catering professional to confirm they are taking care of all food accommodations.
- Know the locations and most direct route to accessible restrooms.
- In the event of an emergency, know where the accessible routes out of the building are located. Do not use elevators in the event of a fire emergency.

Evaluate Your Event

Evaluate the event from an inclusion perspective. It will help you plan your next event. Include these questions in the formal evaluation:

- What accommodations did people request?
- Were the requests received by the due date?
- How did we handle late requests?
- List the accommodations, and how they were made.
- Keep track of the costs of accommodations to help with budgeting for future events.
- Were the event spaces we used, such as parking, building entrances, registration access, main event space, coatroom, and restrooms completely accessible?
- Were requests for accommodations honored by the event location?
- Were the venue's service personnel respectful and easy to work with?
- Were materials available in various formats?
- How many requests did people make for fee accommodations? Where did the funding come from

to cover costs?

ENDNOTES

Chapter 3

[1] Equal Employment Opportunity Commission.
http://www.eeoc.gov/facts/fs-ada.html
[2] Part 35 Nondiscrimination on the Basis of Disability in State and Local Government Services-General Prohibitions Against Discrimination.
https://www.ada.gov/regs2010/titleII_2010/titleII_2010_regulations.htm#a35130
[3] I prefer using Ginny Thornburgh's description "not-apparent disabilities" rather than the more common reference "invisible disabilities."
[4] Pinsky, M.I. There Are No Barriers to God's Love.
http://www.faithformationlearningexchange.net/uploads/5/2/4/6/5246709/no_barriers_to_gods_love.pdf
[5] Deuteronomy *Rabbah* 4:4. Composed in Talmudic Israel/Babylon (900 CE), Deuteronomy Rabbah is a midrash or homiletic commentary.

Chapter 4

[1] Carter, E.W., Kleinert, H.I., LoBianco, T.F., Sheppard-Jones, K., Butler, L.N., Tyree, M.S. (2015). *Congregational Participation of a National Sample of Adults with Intellectual and Developmental Disabilities.* Intellectual and Developmental Disabilities, 53:6, 381-393.
[2] U.S. Census Bureau July, 2012
https://www.census.gov/newsroom/releases/archives/miscellaneous/cb12-134.html

[3] World Report on Disabilities
http://www.who.int/disabilities/world_report/2011/facts
heet.pdf?ua=1

[4] Carter, E.W., et al. p. 391.

[5] World Health Organization, International Classification
of Functioning, Disability and Health, Geneva: World
Health Organization, 2001, p. 214.

[6] Harris Interactive. The ADA, 20 Years Later. Kessler
Foundation/NOD Survey of Americans with Disabilities.
2010. uhttps://www.nod.org/wp-
content/uploads/07c_2010_survey_of_americans_with_di
sabilities_gaps_full_report.pdf.

[7] ADA Checklist for Existing Facilities. New England
ADA Center. https://adachecklist.org/checklist.html

[8] Landsberg, L.F. It's Time to Be Fully Inclusive of Jews
with Disabilities. Reform Judaism.
https://reformjudaism.org/blog/2015/08/05/its-time-be-
fully-inclusive-jews-disabilities

[9] National Collaborative on Workforce and Disability.
Attitudinal Barriers for People with Disabilities.
http://www.ncwd-youth.info

[10] Rife, J.M., Thornburgh, G. *From Barriers to Bridges-A
Community Action Guide for Congregations and People with
Disabilities.* National Organization on Disability, 1996. P.
35.

Chapter 5
[1] Reinders, H. When the World is Falling Apart:
Reflections on the Why? Question. Summer Institute on
Theology and Disability, 2015.

https://www.youtube.com/watch?time_continue=1945&
v=yxhp6YSBVRU9

[2] Adichie, C. N. The Danger of a Single Story, TED Global 2009.
https://www.ted.com/talks/chimamanda_adichie_the_da
nger_of_a_single_story

[3] Katz, N. I've Listened Enough. https://the-art-of-
autism.com/neal-katz/

Chapter 8
[1] ADA Checklist for Existing Facilities. New England
ADA Center. https://adachecklist.org/checklist.html

Chapter 9
[1] Swedeen, B., Cooney, M., Moss, C., Carter, E.W.
Launching Inclusive Efforts Through Community
Conversations-A Practical Guide for Families, Services
Providers, and Communities.
http://www.tennesseeworks.org/wp-
content/uploads/Community-Conversations-Guide-.pdf

Chapter 10
[1] Itturei Torah, translated by Rabbi Neal J. Loevinger,
https://www.myjewishlearning.com/article/body-and-
soul-religion/4

Chapter 11
[1] Portrayal of People with Disabilities. Association of
University Centers on Disabilities (AUCD).
https://www.aucd.org/template/page.cfm?id=605

[2]Introduction to Web Accessibility.
https://www.w3.org/WAI/fundamentals/accessibility-intro/
[3] Making the Web Accessible. https://www.w3.org/WAI/

Chapter 12
[1] Carter, E.W., Taylor, C. E, et. al. Welcoming People with Disabilities and Their Families: A Practical Guide for Congregations, Vanderbilt Kennedy Center, 2014.
[2] Mental Health Facts, National Alliance on Mental Illness (NAMI). https://www.nami.org/Learn-More/Mental-Health-By-the-Numbers

Chapter 13
[1] Kushner, H. *Who Needs God*. Simon and Shuster. 1989, p. 100.
[2] Mental Health Information. National Institute of Mental Health.
https://www.nimh.nih.gov/health/statistics/mental-illness.shtml
[3] Newman, B., Grit, B. *Accessible Gospel, Inclusive Worship*. CreateSpace Independent Publishing Platform, 2016. Barbara Newman has written numerous books on inclusive religious education.
[4] Hall, E. *Now I See the Moon-A Mother, A Son, A Miracle*. Harper Collins. 2010.
[5] Davie, A.R. Thornburgh, G. *That All May Worship: An Interfaith Welcome to People with Disabilities*. Washington, D.C. American Association for People with Disabilities. 2000.

Chapter 15
[1]Twerski, A.J. Schwartz, U. *Positive Parenting: Developing Your Child's Potential*, Mesorah Pubns Ltd. 18996. p. 273.

Chapter 20
[1]Yadamec, C. The Impact of Personalized Organizational Supports on Successful Community Inclusion, The Council on Quality and Leadership (CQL).
[2] U.S. Department of Labor Office of Disability Employment Policy. https://www.dol.gov/odep/
[3]Putting Faith to Work Manual http://faithanddisability.org/projects/putting-faith-to-work/order-putting-faith-to-work-manual/
[4]Jobs Accommodation Network. https://askjan.org/links/ADAtam1.html#V
[5]Olmstead v. LC. Disability Justice. https://disabilityjustice.org/olmstead-v-lc/#cite-note-
[6]How Will Faith Community Services Be Impacted by New CMS Home and Community Based Services Regulations? What *You* as a Leader Should Know. Deborah Fisher, PsyD. Presenter. National Leadership Consortium on Developmental Disabilities University of Delaware.
[7] Carter, L.K. Sharing Her Voice: A Passionate Disability Activist Reflects On Her Work. The New Normal-Blogging Disability. May 11, 2018.

Chapter 21
[1] Mental Health By the Numbers. NAMI. https://www.nami.org/Learn-More/Mental-Health-By-the-Numbers
[2]Risk of Suicide. NAMI https://www.nami.org/Learn-

More/Mental-Health-Conditions/Related-
Conditions/Suicide

[3] Andrade, C. Developing Welcoming Faith Communities:
Inspiring Examples of Faith-Based Initiatives to Help
Individuals with Mental Health Conditions Participate
Fully in the Life of Religious Congregations. The National
Mental Health Consumers Self-Help Clearinghouse. 2015.

[4] Mental Health Myths and Facts
https://www.mentalhealth.gov/basics/mental-health-
myths-facts

[5] Mental Health: A Guide for Faith Community Leaders,
American Psychological Association Foundation, 2016.
psychiatry.org/faith

Chapter 22

[1] Carter, L.K. Sharing Her Voice: A Passionate Disability
Activist Reflects On Her Work. The New Normal-
Blogging Disability. May 11, 2018

[2] Miller, N.B. *Nobody's perfect: Living and growing with children
who have special needs.* Baltimore, MD: Paul H. Brookes.
1994

Chapter 23

[1] Helping People with Intellectual Disabilities Cope with
Loss. Vanderbilt Kennedy Center for Excellence in
Developmental Disabilities.
https://vkc.mc.vanderbilt.edu/assets/files/tipsheets/copi
nglosstips.pdf

[2] Gaines, A.G., Polsky, M.E. *I Have a Question About Death:
A Book for Children with Autism Spectrum Disorders and Other
Special Needs.* Jessica Kingsley Publishers. London, U.K.

2017. https://www.ihaveaquestionbook.com

Appendices
Appendix A
[1] ADA National Network. https://adata.org/faq/what-definition-disability-under-ada

[2] What is the Expanded Definition of "Major Life Activities" Under the ADAAA?
https://www.dol.gov/ofccp/regs/compliance/faqs/ADAfaqs.htm#Q5

Appendix C
[1] Information and Technical Assistance on the Americans with Disabilities Act.
http://www.usdoj.gov/crt/ada/adahom1.htm